The Unexplainable Truth

100 Poems to expand consciousness

By Julian Mann

The Unexplainable Truth

©2017 by Julian Mann. All Rights Reserved

www.julianmann.com
https://www.facebook.com/theunexplainabletruth
https://soundcloud.com/user-243087440

For Louisa and Belle
My Shining Stars

Contents

Section 1: Rhyming Verse

#	Title	Page
1.	Akashic Gardens	14
2.	Angel's Journey	17
3.	Angel's Tear	20
4.	The Beautiful Moment	22
5.	Beautiful	24
6.	Beloved Child	27
7.	Beyond the Form	28
8.	Brighter than the Highest Star	29
9.	Connections	31
10.	The Crystal Throne	33
11.	Descended Master	35
12.	Eagle's Wing	38
13.	Enchanted Forest	40
14.	The Eternal Song	43
15.	A Father's Tears	45
16.	Flying With Angels	48
17.	Focus	50
18.	Gliding	52
19.	The Golden Chalice	54
20.	Happy Birthday to me!	56
21.	I am Your Angel	58
22.	I am With You	61
23.	I Love You	63
24.	Immortal	66
25.	In Between Spaces	69
26.	In Silvery Moonlight	70
27.	Innocent	72
28.	Lake of Knowledge	75
29.	The Matrix of Truth	77
30.	A Moment of Peace	79

31.	Mother	81
32.	A Mother's Tears	83
33.	My Favourite bench	86
34.	Nothing But a Memory	89
35.	Origins	95
36.	Reaching	97
37.	Return to Golden Sun	99
38.	Riding the Tail of a Comet	101
39	Sanctuary	103
40.	Sapphire Flame	106
41.	Silent Knowing	108
42.	Silver Wings	111
43.	Skyline of Dreams	113
44.	Snowy White Peak	115
45.	Temple of Light	117
46.	Tree of Light	119
47.	Undamaged	121
48.	The Unexplainable Truth	127
49.	Voice of God	129
50.	You Are	132

Section 2: Free-flowing poetry

51.	Accepting Light	136
52.	Already Perfect	140
53.	Calm Waves of Love Cannot End	143
54.	The Daisy	145
55.	The Dancer and the Dance	148
56.	Deep Waters	150
57.	The Drawing of a Curtain	152
58.	The Dreamer and the Dream	154
59.	Eternal Shore	156
60.	Fallen	159
61.	Flight of the Great White Eagle	160
62.	Fly With Me	162
63.	The Great Dreamer	164
64.	The Guardian	168
65.	I am Here	170
66.	Lucid Dreamer	171
67.	The Many Coloured Dawn	173
68.	Once Upon a Thought	176
69.	One Light in a Million Hues	179
70.	A Pearlescent Tear	181
71.	Reflections on the Silent River	183
72.	Shores of Evermore	185
73.	Shores of Home	188
74.	Soaring	190
75.	Starlight	192
76.	Surrender	195
77.	Take my Hand	196
78.	Tears of Heaven	199
80.	The Unwavering Vessel	201
81.	Waiting in Twilight	206

Section 3: Sonnets & Haiku

82.	The Blessed Isles	210
83.	The Confines of a Dream	211
84.	Falling Rain	212
85.	Golden Lady	213
86.	The Illusion of Time	214
87.	The Key	215
88.	A Light to Remember	216
89.	The Ocean of Truth	217
90.	One Energy	218
91.	Oneness	219
92.	Quietness	220
93.	Reflections	221
94.	Seven Stars	222
95.	Sleep without Sleeping	223
96.	A Stray Tear	224
97.	Thank you for your Colours	225
98.	Three Parameters	226
99.	Transformation	227
100.	Unreal World	228

Introduction

In January 2017, I was introduced to the Three Principles by my dear friend Carol Boroughs. This had a profound impact on me and I was gifted with life-changing insights. Carol is a Three Principles facilitator. I have known her for over twenty-five years and had been working as her gardener. One day I got curious and slowed down just long enough to ask her about what she does and she offered to spend a day teaching me about it.

With the simplest of phrases, and by the high vibration of her presence, she was able to help me to connect with the deep inner wisdom that lies within each and every one of us. This resulted in profound revelations, which all stemmed simply from a good feeling, a gentle inner knowing that lies beyond words. Little did I know that my kind and unassuming friend happened to be one of the most 'enlightened' people I am ever likely to meet and I will be forever grateful for the blessing of having her as a teacher and friend in my life.

I have been interested in spirituality for most of my adult life. This is not religious spirituality but the kind that accepts the existence of a higher power, God, and the fact that we co-create our realities with that higher power. Whilst the world's religions hold many truths within their teachings, they are sometimes subject to misinterpretation by people. I have read many fascinating books and looked into numerous topics. At the time Carol helped me I was going through a time of great struggle which had pointed me back to the spiritual path.

As I understood that we create our realities from within, I was desperately trying everything I could to improve my situation and it was exhausting! Despite having studied spirituality so much, nothing had ever come close to having the impact that those few hours spent with Carol gave me. Suddenly I did not need to do thousands of affirmations a week, fit in Reiki and meditation, do EFT, study abundance books and more, all whilst working all the hours just trying to keep my family fed and housed! I could do these things if I felt like it but I did not *need* to do them anymore. Suddenly I was the source! It's a continuing process of deepening understanding but at the core of it is the realisation that we are all already perfect and healed and the answers we seek are already within us.

Looking back, I can see that all the events in my life and everything I had learned had prepared me for that moment. The universe truly does work in perfect ways. I had asked/ prayed for help and it came in ways I could never have imagined. Once we are able to get out of God's way and accept that a loving intelligence far greater than our limited selves is out there helping us, we open the door that allows miracles to manifest in our lives.

Some of the spiritual teachings I had held as absolutes turned out to be only temporary assumptions (beliefs) based on my understanding at the time. Other teachings were transformed from being concepts I had learned about on an intellectual level to being deep inner understandings that I not only understood but simply 'knew' at a deep level. There are unlimited layers of understanding and awareness on the way back to our true selves. Our true self is divine light and might be referred to as 'Higher self' or 'Christ within'. Whatever you choose to call it, the true self is magnificent, unlimited and made from pure love. This is the love of God of which we are all a part.

Almost immediately after Carol helped me, I came across Michael Mirdad through Facebook. That is to say that once my consciousness changed, I reflected another teacher. Michael is a well-known spiritual teacher that encourages the awakening of Christ consciousness within each of us. He is well-versed in 'A

Course in Miracles' and has a vast knowledge of all things spiritual. He radiates love and kindness, balanced by wisdom and reflecting him in my life is yet another blessing for which, once again, I am deeply grateful. I received further insights from listening to Michael. Watching his broadcasts often results in a state of heightened awareness and connection to that beautiful inner feeling that guides us back home.

I first met Roger Blackiston through the Facebook group 'Friends of Michael Mirdad'. Roger is a beautiful and loving person and is also a prolific and highly talented poet, author and magician, to name but a few of his many talents! He writes deeply moving poetry, much of which reaches for spiritual truth. I published my first rhyming poem 'Silent Knowing' on the Friends of Michael Mirdad Facebook page and was greatly encouraged by Roger who invited me to join his Facebook poetry group 'Forest of Song'. Here I was able to continually post my poetry long after we had to limit the amount of poetry we shared on Friends of Michael Mirdad because we were overwhelming the group which is not just about poetry. Forest of Song has continued to grow and is blessed with a myriad of talented poets. The beautiful synchronicity of these events is a wonderful reflection of the fact that the universe is perfect, friendly and loving, and Roger reflecting in my life is yet another thing for which I am deeply grateful.

As a result of these life-changing experiences, I found that I was aflame with energy and inspiration and I had an overwhelming desire to share these gifts of consciousness that I had received. However, these gifts are basically a good feeling, an inner knowing that we are perfect beings made from love and light, that the trials and challenges of life are a powerful illusion that temporarily blinds us to the truth of our own divinity. This 'knowing' brings feelings of peace and trust which in turn generates good feelings and beautiful thoughts that help us to create a beautiful life. When challenges do present in our lives, this inner trust helps us to stay centred and to be at peace, aware of the underlying beauty in every moment, even when the outer circumstances of our lives are difficult. Thus we are able to return to peace more quickly and from that place of peace and trust, we are able to continue to create a beautiful life automatically.

There is no trying, there is only knowing, a knowing that lies deep within us all, that we can connect with just because it is always there, it is already the truth of who we are.

Fear, pain and suffering are in fact an illusion, albeit a very powerful one. All of our emotions come only from our thoughts and when negative feelings come, we have the power to let the associated negative thoughts pass us by like pieces of driftwood floating harmlessly by down the stream of our consciousness. So it is that even when life presents us with challenges (and it will), you always have the power to find your way back to the peace at the centre of your being. It is, in fact, possible to find peace even when you are experiencing a low mood. Understanding this truth at a deep level is what lights the way back to the home we never left.

There are many insights I have wanted to share but insight is not something you can give away because it comes from a formless inner truth that lies beyond the form of words and exists as a good feeling.

Shortly after my experience, I became overwhelmed by words and images in my mind that compelled me to find a way to express myself. Having never considered myself to be a poet I suddenly found I could not stop the endless flow of words that came flooding through, as though a dam had burst within me, causing an unstoppable outflowing of creative expression.

These good feelings, that are borne of the light and love within us, cannot be explained, they can only be expressed through metaphor in the hope that this will help the reader connect with this 'Unexplainable Truth'.

Poetry is a wonderful medium for sharing this deep inner truth. When you read my poems, look for that good feeling above all else. Don't try to work it out with your intellect, this truth lies beyond your personal mind. If you can get quiet and feel that good feeling, then you have connected with the beauty and truth within your own being and my poems have served their purpose.

If reading the poems helps you to connect with the silent wisdom within you then you may receive your own insights. If this should happen, just be grateful for it and return to the peaceful, good feeling. We are all conditioned to employ our intellects to work everything out. Whilst the intellect is an amazing tool, it serves no purpose here because the intellect is a tool of the form and this silent peace, love and wisdom come from a formless place.

It is the good feeling that is connecting you to the deep inner truth of your being, in a place beyond form where unlimited wisdom is available, in the silence where there is only love.

Section 1

Rhyming Verse

'In the silence of our minds lies creative incubation, bringing the wisdom and the joy we all seek'
Sydney Banks

Akashic Gardens

I pause in my long day's labour,
From a duty filled with love,
To look up and see such splendour,
In the light-filled rows above.

To take a moment and stroll outside,
To the gardens, I know so well.
I have tended these grounds with love and sweet pride,
There are so many stories to tell.

I glide down winding paths of crystal,
Past the drifts of amethyst dreams,
Through the radiant Unicorn's stables,
Where all around true healing beams.

Looking in silence for my special grove,
A place I created where my cares I can steal
Away, in radiant pearl shards of love,
Where it's only peace that I feel.

My dearest beloved, you helped me create,
This garden of radiant light,
That lifts us up into a heavenly state,
As we are enveloped in a beauty so bright.

Welcome dearest heart to awaken,
In this special and secret place.
Where the foundations of fear are quietly shaken,
And all the cares dissolve from your face.

Here in the light garden the crystals reach up to Heaven's ceiling,
Like beautiful trees miles high and ancient,
Radiating peace and such a beautiful feeling,
That heals all levels till there's only the present.

The one true time and the only true state,
To which the mighty light trees connect you.
Their radiant presence so sublime and great,
You know you are love whatever you do.

I sit upon my favourite bench of cedar,
By a fountain of sparkling pure water,
Shaded by ferns and stocks of the night,
Scented with love in this most private corner.

Where I have consulted the Master of Light,
As we leaned on lapis balustrades on the edge of time,
And now I look out at my heart's favourite sight,
Of infinity's fields of loving divine.

This place is so special and personal to me,
I co-created it in innocent, sweet reverie.
A special and timeless corner of sanctuary,
Where all my being exists in love's harmony.

And so I pray to always remember,
This state that lives inside my dreams.
And when I would feel this love so tender,
I can return here on a light beam.

And gaze at the stars set in indigo sky
At the comets and galaxies painting a heavenly view
Where shining hosts of angels fly
And I return to the one state that's true.

Angel's Journey

An Angel gliding effortlessly,
Over the unending ocean,
Seeking a shoreline to the land where souls rest peacefully,
Soaring so high, the solitary flight of one.

The waves ripple as light reflections,
Of the indigo sky above,
Peppered with stars and divine emanations,
Glowing in the living tapestry of love.

Will this ocean lead me home?
Over these crystal clear waters, pure and ancient?
To the place where I cannot feel alone,
Where peace and love resound yet silent.

There it is, the distant land,
A glowing beach as long as the unlimited horizon.
The beauty of golden and pink sand,
The place where all sing, loved as one.

And beyond the golden pink shore,
Lush and verdant forests of plenty,
Where none could want for more,
And all shines with such great beauty.

Gliding home the angel reaches the shore and feels complete,
His faith never wavered, he knew he could only come home,
He longs to land and feel the warm sands beneath his feet,
Yet instinct tells him his journey is not yet done.

Onward he soars,
Over the verdant forest so vibrant and lush.
The joyful fairies offer him applause!
Bathed in love, his mind enters a peaceful hush.

Flying over great waterfalls of light,
Cascading down the rising lands,
Rainbow mist forms a beautiful sight,
The angel feels the mist with his outstretched hands.

Open and receptive to all the beauty and good,
Feeling complete, full of joy, full of life,
Knowing that here none can be misunderstood,
For, in these lands there is only love, never strife.

His outstretched wings delighted with surprise,
As they pick up the rising updrafts,
There before him, the great mountains rise,
Their healing peaks wash away the illusion of past.

So majestic, these peaks rise to the heavens,
Their snow-capped crowns sparkling with glorious radiance,
Shining and promising new wisdom given,
That all things joined are part of one dance.

The air currents, warm with the winds of love,
The angel's spirit lifts.
As he is gently guided to Heaven above,
And into a higher vibration, he shifts.

So safe and warm and satisfied,
Without resistance, upward flying,
His heart swelling with love, so gratified!
Heading home without even trying.

Soaring over the heavenly peaks he spots a shining beacon,
Sat upon the highest peak, radiating golden light,
This is the doorway that leads beyond,
Where all illusions melt from sight.

Resolutely the angel soars towards this divine portal,
That expands to his entire field of vision,
Filling up with bliss, as one with all,
At last the angel completes his mission.

For he has returned to the one true place,
That he never left, where we all are now,
Existing as light a state of heavenly grace,
One day this angel, we all will follow.

Angel's Tear

An angel's tear drops silently,
Kissed by Heaven's rays,
Falling effortlessly,
Into the golden ocean to stay.

A myriad of colour,
Of joyful thanks and praise,
For the fortune of our splendour,
Into holy light we raise.

This vast expanse of timeless hope,
Into which our fondest dreams elope.
The sadness of a long lost love,
Is healed as one on an azure cove.

Reflecting Heaven, the silent surface,
Glistening, peaceful truths.
'Knowing' is the gift we purchase,
Seeing our divinity is proof.

What dreams caress the breath of God?
Beneath the surface laying
Waiting for quiet discovery, she nods,
The ancient mother praying.

That all her children, beautiful and free,
As diamond stardust in the void,
Will one day come to simply be,
The love of Heaven deployed.

With violet perfume in the breeze,
She waits for time to end.
In a swaying bed, of lavender joy, we ease,
Our inner light extends.

Her golden wings so vast and shimmering,
Gliding grace over lakes of peace,
Our hearts, our very souls enveloping,
In unending seas of blossoms released.

The silence waits beyond this form so new,
It's peace as clear as crystal.
Crimson raindrops of the dawn of knowing's dew,
Are with us now as one are all.

Let no other speak of loss,
Or yield to so-called 'separation',
Or think our fate is left to the toss,
Of a coin of our damnation!

Titans soaring into the vast expanse,
Of the heavens' infinite span,
Is what we are in present tense,
Shards of light in God's great plan!

The Beautiful Moment

As I pause in this moment of beauty,
Radiating peace into this world,
Laying gently down in fields of plenty,
Diving into the deep truth untold.

As I lie in this instant of timeless wonder,
Shining unbridled joy into this dream,
And I gaze into the indigo firmament,
Filled with a trillion light beams.

I sink inside and stop the play,
Unhindered silence rises up,
There is stunning perfection here every day,
Unlimited love fills up my cup.

Just stopping still on the twilit edge of eternity,
To hear the silent song revealed,
That we are love and perfect beauty,
It is always there under thoughts concealed.

These thoughts are a gift, with which we can shape our dream,
We need not stop them nor could we even try,
Let them pass by as a lazy canoe on a quiet, sunlit stream,
Then into your true nature let your spirit fly.

The peace we all search for is already there in conclusion
It is the truth of our being, we are radiant light!
Beneath mind's chatter, beyond the distraction,
The golden silence reveals our might.

In every moment staggering beauty,
Dazzling starlight awakens the sleeping horizon,
For there is only this instant of perfect eternity
In the bliss of our true state as part of the one.

To find it, abandon your search, beloved light,
Because this illusion has blinded your sight,
That which you seek you already are,
It is inside, not outside, my infinite star.

Beautiful

When I look into your eyes,
I see your soul so filled with light.
I see a being that is so high,
And I am staggered by the sight,
Of something truly beautiful.

How could I ever see something wrong?
When inside of you such exquisite form,
Is created from the hummingbird's song
So graceful, infinite, light and warm.
Oh my, you are so beautiful!

When I listen to your words,
I feel the joy of a divine chorus.
In my heart, I feel love surge,
It comes from you and me and us.
You are so very beautiful!

Behind the form that stands before me,
I see an angel filled with love.
Deep inside I sense your story,
And so I feel the peace of the dove.
And it is simply beautiful!

Your light shines forth in multi-coloured rays.
Your light filled essence shines always.
I am stunned and just amazed,
By the love and the light behind your gaze,
It's serene sun-filled love and it is beautiful!

How could I judge you, doubt you or steal
My love for you, when all I see
Is that your essence is love, that's all that's real,
It's there behind your humanity,
Perfect and beautiful.

When the world falls into disarray,
When we lose sight of our true destination,
That is the time to gather and pray,
To remember we all are one creation,
And we are beautiful!

I am so filled with gratitude,
Because as I walk down the street,
I am blessed with heavenly attitude,
And I see light in everyone I meet,
My goodness, you are all so beautiful!

Inside every one of us,
There flies a heavenly host.
We are made of light and stardust,
They sing how we are loved the most.
A diamond love bird chanting 'You are beautiful!'

When angel's tears burst into form,
A many-coloured rainbow,
That sees that we shall weather the storm,
Because inside the light we know,
That we are beautiful!

A flying starling soars into the sky,
Sprinkling stardust from on high.
The heavens wonder, the light beings sigh,
The holy mother gives a joyful sigh,
And cries 'My children are so beautiful!'

We were made from the light above,
A billion shards of purest love.
When we can remember the blissful truth,
We shall see the radiant proof-
We are staggeringly beautiful!

We are made of God; we are beings of light,
Innocent flowers swaying gently,
In the warm safe breeze of an angel's flight,
Golden sun rays on fields of plenty.
Stunningly beautiful!

So never let your heart feel doubt,
Your brothers and sisters are love so pure.
Growing into one is what we are about,
We need never feel insecure
Because God sees us, and we are beautiful.

If Heaven cracked open and love burst forth,
Into every corner of creation,
We'd light the sky from South to North,
And give Heaven back salvation.
Because we are God and we are beautiful.

Beloved Child

Beloved child who walks in light,
Know that I am with you for every joyful step, so light-footed,
Never shall you leave my sight,
For, you are the treasure in which the future is rooted.

So brightly burns your shining star,
And I would cherish every sacred moment of you,
From your side, I am never far,
Whispering how my love for you is true.

And I anoint you with the golden cup of cherished ages,
As even now I am stunned by your perfection,
Today's beloved children are tomorrow's sages,
So I would enrich you with gentle revelation.

How fiercely beats with pride my open heart!
For you are beauty and sweet salvation,
With joyful eyes I see you heal that which fell apart,
With gentle forgiveness, you bring unification.

How can I express my devotion and love,
For you my cherished one?
I watch over you from heaven above,
So thrilled to see all the good you've done.

Your value cannot be given proper measure,
Because you are too special for these feeble words.
You are God's joy, his divine treasure,
The pride and joy of your one Lord.

Beyond the Form

There is a place beyond the form,
Of clear calm waters before the storm,
This is a peaceful energy,
Where my rested soul can stay.

This peace and light is my one truth,
I need only be quiet to find the proof,
I am infinite light beaming through the heavens,
Flowing as a river through beautiful canyons.

This energy is pure love, essentially perfect,
If I can get out of my way then that is what I reflect,
It's deep in my core before all the lessons,
Before all the acts that must be forgiven.

If I could connect to this truth that is me,
Then I would break illusions chains and fly joyfully free,
They say I am here to learn lessons from above,
But what need of lessons has the essence of pure love?

When I am still and listen to the silence,
Unlimited wisdom is my infinite presence,
I am heavenly stardust, love's golden beam,
An expression of infinity, immersed in a dream.

Brighter Than the Highest Star

So softly falls the white dove's feather,
Shimmering in moon rays,
Against the clear night sky in the yearning desert,
In the silken light of always.

I have treasured your time with me my beloved,
On this ocean of one and a billion pearls,
Of wisdom and long forgotten dreams,
Washed up on the eternal shore, yet never removed.

Come bathe with me in this warm sea under midnight sky,
Floating against the dark backdrop of a trillion lights,
Waiting for heavenly dawn to light our way,
That we might look forward to where God sets our sights.

This water so gently warm embracing me,
Enveloping me in the dream of a thousand sweet memories,
Of timeless moments, lived joyfully,
Of daydreams gifted lovingly.

Feel my heart light shining upon you,
With unending love so bright and true,
Your gifts too precious, you golden prize,
You beautiful sky with crimson sunrise.

I waited here long years, a thousand score,
Knowing our love would be forevermore,
Sensing our truth as a glittering galaxy,
Of light and love for all to see.

Will you share my cup Beloved Light?
I would fill it with the honeyed nectar of plenty,
Enough to lift all souls to flight
And shine this love upon all we see.

You are eternal light,
A prophetic vision.
A glorious sight
With a divine mission.

To shower all this world with love,
To make on Earth the heavens move,
For how could you ignite my sky of eternal hope,
Before we join form in our dream to elope?

I would only wish you an eternal sun,
A flock of shimmering lovebirds adorning your sky,
May your dream be light filled love and fun,
May you only tears of joy, ever cry.

I see you as the divine light that you are,
Shining brighter than Heaven's highest star!
I wait so calmly for your acceptance in this moment
So that for our love the angels can be present.

I see you with my open heart,
I hear you with my deepest feeling,
I cannot wait for this new journey to start,
In this Eden where the world has healing.

Connections

Deep inside, behind the busy chatter,
Lies consciousness divine,
This pure love is all that matters,
It will change your world by God's design.

You need not strain to figure things out,
Or try to change another,
All goodness shall come about,
If this truth you can rediscover.

When you connect with this pure love,
That is the truth of who we are,
You find quiet peace on the wings of the dove,
You shine your golden inner star.

Just slowing down and dropping unwanted thought,
Is all you need to find your peace,
By seeking without looking for what you've sought,
You will bring this sweet relief.

There's nothing to do,
No plan to put in place,
Just find the truth of you,
And let go of any race.

Changing within by becoming what you are,
Is all you need to do,
No effort strain or scheming that's bizarre,
Just relax and still be you.

For when you find this peace inside,
Something happens that is astounding,
Your loved ones will see the world with new eyes,
Because of the love consciousness, you are resounding!

All we need do is find our truthful centre,
To begin this beautiful transformation,
Then into our lives, this love can enter,
It's there already, this divine inspiration!

Because we are all one,
We are all connected,
We are light beams from the same Sun.
So when one of us finds their thinking corrected.

Then the one Sun can rise,
So all the other light beams will shine the same way,
And this love we shall see with our eyes.
There is nothing else you need do or say.

The Crystal Throne

I sit upon my crystal throne,
In the ancient hall of ageless instants,
Above rise walls of pearl and alabaster,
Stretching up unending into the infinite Sun.

Angels circle high above,
Their wings a glittering spectacle of iridescent beauty,
Into our hearts, they radiate pure love,
Tis the joy of God, and not a duty.

Aloft I hold this world of passing reflections,
Within my very hands,
A place of unlimited wonders, hidden within distractions,
The key to peaceful distant lands.

I raise this world up into the light,
Bathing it in angelic radiance,
Healing war, and pain and plight,
In the shining rays of God light brilliance.

And so my task is underway,
A golden drop of hope in an ocean of uncertainty,
For raising consciousness I pray,
That we may transcend ego's insanity.

I would return to that quiet rose garden,
In our special place beneath the stars,
Where it is warm and safe with deep compassion,
And the silken veil of love covers all that is near and far.

I look out into the vastness of unending skies,
Burning cerise in the Dawn of Salvation,
Where the dove of peace with angels flies,
And all as one join in perfection.

That silent symphony that holds our birthright,
As it is sung by a heavenly chorus,
That tells us we are love and light,
Unblemished perfection is the truth of us.

And so I leave this chamber of dreaming,
To walk with my beloveds beneath the curtain of fond hopes,
A billion star lights with beauty beaming,
As every heart into pure love elopes.

Descended Master

As I glide through halls of timeless light,
In the eternal temple on the edge of the nightingale's kiss,
I reach out my arms, my fingertips caress,
Smooth pillars of marble, embroidered with bliss.

Gliding effortlessly into the Archangels' flight,
My mind at one with the thousand-petaled lotus blossom.
In this place, I feel all divine insight,
That enraptures me with joy as illusion is forgotten.

Emboldened by truth, my heart bursting with love,
That pours forth into the gilded corners of creation.
I stand as proof that mountains can move,
When diamond-lined intentions are set into motion.

I reach the courtyard of my soul's fondest dreams,
With lapis lazuli cobbles in a circle of light,
A host of my dearest loves part ways and then beam
Golden rays of love, 'tis a heavenly sight.

Arches of ancient wisdom tower upwards in graceful ornament,
Gently framing this circle bathing in heavenly sky,
Their gleaming pearl structure in beautiful firmament,
Is there to enhance love's eternal supply.

I have all I need and I rest safely home,
I lie in golden ploughed meadows in fields of Elysium,
At one with pure bliss, I am never alone,
But service to love presents a conundrum.

For I have climbed the mountain of dreams and conquered its summit,
I rest with the Angels in swaying lavender groves in the valleys of light,

And yet I would serve and back into the dream choose to plummet,
So that I might share my love and help end my lost siblings' plight.

Oh yes, it all seems simple enough,
When your essence is at one with the bliss.
You see the eternal picture and so return to the rough,
Asleep in a dark dream, your home shall you miss.

And how should you stay in this dream already transcended?
I took a heavy anchor made from ego's dark matter,
An illusion already dissolved that before I had ended,
Embraced as a chain of judgment that would act as a tether.

So that I might remain in that divine illusion once again,
And risk a lifetime of confusion and pain.
All to serve the light and help raise Earth's vibration,
To help put an end to suffering I have resumed my station.

Yet all that I know I have once again forgotten,
I have now the chance to remember love's truth.
If I don't manage to remember I risk re-joining the wheel,
Of illusory karma and the so-called need to heal.

Swimming in murky waters, a lost light of perfection,
How may I filter this muddied quagmire?
And purify this illusion of cold separation,
And once again move past all earthly desire?

The anchor will drive me insane there's no doubt!
But that's the only way for me to stay here.
So, remembering my light is the only way out,
As is seeing the love that dissolves all the fear.

But in my soul, the memory is freed from its casting,
Of those golden-lit halls in the Light Master's temple,
On the edge of forever in that moment of bliss everlasting,
Somehow I would know I am divine vessel.

In the greater light of one, it really matters not,
For we all will return to the one place we are.
Although that is of little consolation when ego thickens the plot,
And from the light, you feel flung afar.

Yet I am a master, a being of light!
I have ascended that dream and spread my wings in flight!
I will unfold them again in midst of the dream,
And enfold my beloveds in a golden light beam.

I am here to serve, for that is what counts,
There is nothing beyond love that matters.
And so from my conquered peak I dismount
To help heal a world that's in tatters.

Eagle's Wing

When the tip of the great eagle's wing
Caresses the sky,
When a host of heavenly angels sing,
And pure tears of joy I cry.

I sit in solace beneath the open sky,
My very soul unwrapped in unobstructed light,
My heart has wings that let me fly,
Into the beauty of God's sight.

So I wait, pondering my existence,
Contemplating my challenges,
A futile chore at my ego's insistence,
If I would look through truthful lenses.

The answer always lies within,
In the quiet mind,
It's my busy mind that does my head in,
That sees a world harsh and unkind.

In the quiet mind the truth surfaces,
As with the floor of the silent ocean,
Where ever-present hidden instances,
Have lain within us since before time began.

I still my heart and find the centre,
My truth is peace in the eye of a storm,
That never happened, for love is gentler,
Than the hustle and bluster in the dream of form.

So here I drift free from heart's yearning,
A shimmering butterfly in moonlight silhouetted,
As love-light perfection, illusion is learning,
As we are reflections of God, in pure love created!

Enchanted Forest

Our divine song became enraptured,
In summer breeze on meadow scented blossoms.
In which a timeless moment captured,
Led us to this peaceful sanctuary uncommon.

I walk with the night, the ancient moon as my guide,
I find the sacred forest where the tree spirits hide,
The path opens before me as though the laden branches sigh,
And beckon me into a world where emerald forest is sky.

I come to an arch made of branches woven as wicker,
In the silent still dark I see tiny rainbow lights flicker,
Suddenly they coalesce into a form divinely beautiful,
And I am asked 'Will you pass with a heart of love that is full?'

The shimmering light being fills me with harmony,
I feel light as a feather carried on the warmed winds,
Of love that flows into a place that is higher,
Where there's joy and there's laughter and dancing by fire.

Thank you, Great Spirit of this forest enchanted,
For letting me enter your valley of lilies,
As I glide past the banks of pure white birches,
I see the tiniest and brightest most curious faces!

I feel so very honoured to be allowed in this place,
I am here as a favour granted in grace.
As I am guided further into this emerald light realm,
I know that I am not at the helm!

I release all control to these spirits beneficent,
And I stumble across a sight quite magnificent!
As I am guided past an iridescent crystal grove,
I am treated to a view which forever I will love!

A tree so ancient, so beautiful and light,
That my breath is taken away by this wonderful sight!
This mighty being reaches miles up high!
And joins the Earth to the heavenly sky.

In the centre of the trunk there now appears a doorway,
Its warm energy beckons me and I cannot resist,
I walk through this portal and the night turns to day,
And on in my journey, I must now persist.

Before me unfolds the most incredible sight,
A secret kingdom of the fairy and the elf and the sprite.
Glass towers of honeysuckle reaching up to the Sun.
And a smile of joy on the face of everyone.

Great flowers in a myriad of colours so new,
That I am in joyful tears at this wondrous view,
Such beauty I see that I am filled with ecstatic bliss,
How fortunate am I to this glory witness?

I ask the Elf queen: 'How comes you are here?'
She says with a smile that portrays only love
'We've always been close by to you my sweet dear,
You just couldn't see us till you gave your ego the shove!'

And so I spent many hours of light,
Dancing and singing and setting things right,
I offered my love and received it back a hundredfold,
It's deeper than words and cannot be told.

'Come and see us again when next its full moon,
But leaves your cares and controls far behind.
We can't wait to play and laugh with you soon
Now that you have healed your beautiful mind.'

The Eternal Song

I take a breath and slow my mind,
I pause and quiet my busy chatter,
For in this space is a love so kind,
That none of my cares really seem to matter.

I slow it down, to the rhythm of my heart,
Letting go of my needs and concerns,
Connecting with higher energy of which I am a part,
Uncovering the peace for which my consciousness yearns.

There it is, behind the distractions,
A beautiful presence that was there all along,
The constant drum of God's heartbeat in all its perfection,
This is the sound of the Eternal Song.

This peace, this beauty, this divine light,
Is within us wherever we go,
We have only to quieten to find this insight,
That the answer to all questions, we already know.

There in the silence, where the eagle's feather gently falls,
Where angelic choirs sing with heavenly voice,
Where the master of light to our gentle soul calls,
To tell us that we have unlimited choice.

Quieten down, my sweetest love,
Your joy is always near,
Let go and find the peace of the dove,
Just listen in the quietness and the truth you will hear.

There is nothing to do,
Nothing to work out,
Because perfection is you,
Of this truth never doubt.

A Father's Tears

With gentle strength and soft caress,
You made me feel so safe.
I cannot begin to fully express,
The beauty of that state.

You always strived
To make it work,
You helped me thrive,
You never shirked.

My love for you is with you now
With such thanks and gratitude.
I look at you and marvel how
You had such loving attitude!

My Father dear I love you so,
On Earth, I completed my time.
I'm sorry that I had to go,
But I'm still here as you are mine.

If you should crumble filled with grief,
Then please take stock and know,
Let this truth bring some relief,
I'm in your heart somehow.

You see this world so full of tears,
But this is just a scene,
Beyond the thinnest veil of fears,
We bask in love's full beam!

When you are hurting deep inside,
Yet outwardly remain
So strong you fill me up with pride,
Your strength is not in vain.

For as you stay a light of strength,
To keep your loved ones safe and sound,
Please know I'll go to any length,
To show you that by love we're bound.

I live as light in peace and bliss,
I have returned to home,
And whatever happens, I promise you this,
I am never alone.

So take heart, my wonderful Dad,
My warrior for light,
When you feel the grief too bad,
I want to make it right.

We only stay a short sojourn,
In this passing breeze called life,
There really is no need to mourn,
Because we move beyond all strife.

To a place that's warm and filled with bliss,
The purest form of love,
And that is why you must not miss,
The freedom flying dove.

That rises with my very soul,
To guide me back to peace,
I am here and there and everywhere,
Hold this truth as belief.

Because beyond the pain in gentle flight,
This truth can now resound,
That we are love born of the light,
And all are homeward bound.

So thank you gentle Father dear,
So loyal and so true,
As one with all, I'm always near,
And I'm shining love on you.

Flying with Angels

I sit with Angels at the foot of the Great Tree,
Its mighty branches reaching up into an infinite sky,
Its girth so vast, it is more than I can see,
We sing to the music of harps as we prepare to fly.

Up, up, upwards and onwards!
Past layers of lichen-encrusted beauty!
To see all this splendour we must first look inwards,
For it is within that our spirit flies free.

Soaring on through conscious elevation,
Past so many miles of luscious green leaf,
We pause on the threshold of perfect elation,
We alight on emerald boughs to take sweet relief.

We drink the honeyed nectar from the fruit of first awakening,
Such sweetness softens our grateful lips,
At last aware of our long night's dreaming,
We continue to drink with ecstatic sips.

Now so refreshed we prepare to journey on,
The heavenly music continues,
I am wrapped in the pure joy of this heavenly song,
And a quiet acceptance of all that ensues.

Upward we rise alongside phoenix and albatross,
Above the heavenly canopy,
To a dreamscape of light where nothing is lost,
A realm of rainbows and beauty.

A crystal clear curtain over an indigo backdrop,
Peppered with a billion star-lights,
Paint the sky with unlimited promise,
And so we continue our joy-filled flight.

Onward we glide over temples of Heaven,
With gardens of fuchsia and lavender,
Where hummingbirds dance with love freely given,
And hearts are filled with a love that is tender.

Then we see it in the distance aglow!
On the edge of the unending horizon!
In to a vermillion, sunset is where we shall go!
A heavenly gateway back to the true state of one!

In the soft warm wind my eyes for joy weep,
For now, all my cares have dissolved,
I'm returning to the one place where we awaken from our sleep,
We are all going home and we are truly beloved.

Focus

Focus:
On pink white sands and azure waters,
A special holiday in paradise,
A time of joy with your sons and your daughters,
Seeing happiness and joy in your loved ones' eyes.

Focus:
On summer in the mountains, drinking from the clearest cool spring,
On oceans of wildflowers swaying in the freshly perfumed breeze,
On the delights of this world that make your heart sing,
As you blissfully manifest a joyous life with ease.

Focus:
On all you have, the great and the small,
Your home, your car, your living.
Even if you think you've got not much at all,
Say 'Thanks for all the giving'.

Focus:
On love and light and days of laughter,
For you have seen such sun-kissed happiness,
As down the stream of your life, you lazily saunter,
And on your mind your good fortune you impress.

Focus:
On all you've learned because you've come so far,
Now feel your heart swell with gratitude!
You once were dreamed upon a star,
And now you shine with your loving attitude.

Focus:
A brand new car, a home improvement,
All that you want can be yours now and more,
For as you give your thought to the firmament,
So shall you see your intentions coming ashore.

Focus:
On a world of light that knows only peace,
Where all beloved people are awakened,
To their own divinity as their fear they release,
And into a higher vibration of love, Humanity is taken.

Focus:
Choose wisely your thoughts that create your feelings this day,
Dearest co-creator of life, made from divine light magnificent,
And forget any times that you wandered astray,
'Now' is the moment that makes all the difference.

Gliding

Gliding on the Wings of Infinity,
Spanning the Horizon of Forever,
Chasing the twilight 'oer the Shores of Eternity,
Reaching for the crimson treasure.

Indigo peace engulfs my being, it is inevitable,
Might I catch one final ray of eternal lifeblood?
My thirst for beauty is unquenchable,
My heart sings for joy as all I see is good.

The silent spectre of beyond-form,
Stunning my mind into the glistening stillness,
Of the lake that never ends on the edge of a scarlet dawn,
I take my leave to be reabsorbed into allness.

Still gliding, without even a whisper, I am,
I drift into the enchanted emerald forest,
Effortlessly passing the titanic trunks of the ancient guardians,
Past timeless drifts of a million fireflies, my heart opens in earnest.

Their fire-glowing beauty as profound as any expression,
Of the divine source unleashed in full swing.
Such beauty, grace and illumination,
I bathe in light as angels sing.

There was no end insight,
For the quietly gliding traveller.
Wait for me where dusk becomes night,
And share my cup, beloved brother.

And sister too, my beacon of beauty and grace,
I cherish your wings of gold.
I look into your eyes and see God's face,
I surrender, allowing my own story to unfold.

The Golden Chalice

I hold the Golden Chalice aloft,
Rivers of light and iridescent beams of love flow over its edges,
Bejewelled with stardust sparkling and soft,
How many times have I supped from its wisdom?

This sacred vessel of light,
That holds the secret key,
It shines a love so bright,
One sip and I am free!

To soar across unending galaxies,
Ancient beauty stretching across my view,
Catching the luminescent tail of a comet,
And seeing all that is old is new.

This cup that holds the great ocean,
Of all that is and ever could be,
That answers all questions of what I am,
And simply says that you are me.

I would not wait another moment to quietly drink,
So I lift the chalice to my grateful lips, and silently I imbibe,
Of wisdom without limits that speaks beneath all that which I think,
That ushers forth from a love that my words cannot describe.

Where might I go now in this crystallized moment?
Bending the very laws of time,
I can travel the eternal ocean of my heart's content,
For cleared of all debris is the path to the divine.

All it takes is a single quiet moment,
To feel the connection that is already there,
That beholds all wisdom in a magical instant,
And releases the golden dragon from his lair.

To soar upward exhilarated and free,
To ignite the distant skies in crimson flames,
Burning so brightly that everything I can see,
And with the humblest gratitude, I can break my chains.

Gently I lift up the silken curtain of night,
So thin and finely woven,
By the master craftsmen from the Temple of Light,
To hear the voice of truth, so silently spoken.

I rest my soul upon infinity's star,
And feel my inner connection,
For this is the truth of what we all are,
Rays of light from the golden sun of perfection.

Happy Birthday to Me!

Happy birthday to me!
In this last year, I flew free,
For I was blessed with such deep healing,
That I was connected to that blissful feeling.

Which is the only true state,
That lies beyond Heaven's gate,
The only true place,
As a sparkle on Gods face!

How may I express,
My heartfelt thankfulness,
For all the help I have been given,
To remember from divine light we are riven.

I saw that time does not exist,
That there is only now that's real,
So no longer can past hurts persist,
In an instant, we can heal.

I learned that thought is always there,
An endless stream of energy,
But we don't have to react at all,
If those thoughts are less than summery!

I met with Christ who helped me let go,
Of my reticence to help, thinking it was pride.
In the light, I was shown it was just my ego,
Hoping my light I would hide.

So now I gladly make the choice,
To be a channel for Heaven's voice,
And If I can help but for a moment,
It will fill my heart with great content.

It's happened so fast, it seems unreal,
But that has been another lesson,
Because this life has an illusory feel,
It's a divine dream in session.

I see the glimmers of new insight,
That our bodies are really made of light,
That space and time do not exist,
And our little ego's, the truth resist.

I feel such love for life and all,
With passion and excitement, I meet each day,
And with my next chapter my mind I enthral,
I found my way home and I am here to stay.

I Am Your Angel

Always with you,
Never far,
Whatever you should say or do,
You will be my shining star

Waiting with my wings outstretched,
Ready to enfold you,
If you should ever need my help,
To you, I am forever true.

I whisper in your ear by night,
Telling you of all my love,
Seeing that you are higher light,
A gift of beauty from above.

Never would I leave your side,
My most dearly beloved prize,
I look to you and fill with pride,
When I see the soul light in your eyes.

You are a treasure beyond form or expression,
A diamond refracting the everlasting rainbow,
I'm here to help you with your mission,
And from your life, I'll never go.

When you feel down,
Small and frightened,
I'll place on your head your golden crown,
And help you feel enlightened.

To love you, hold you and cherish your light,
Is what I am here to do.
I'll help you spread your own wings in flight,
And I will always shine love upon you.

So if you need me remember I'm here,
I am so close by, waiting for your permission.
I'll shine divine love to dissolve all your fear,
Gently awaking you is my mission.

I must always respect that you have your free will,
So please remember to ask,
Because to help you out gives me such a thrill!
For it is my most sacred task.

You are always loved!
You are never alone!
I help you to soar with the eagle and dove,
I want to bring you home.

My most precious gem, such a beautiful sight!
My deepest pride and golden joy,
My light beam of love pure and bright,
I am your angel and I am in your employ.

So reach out and ask to feel my love,
I'll shower you with peace and light,
You are the pride of my treasure trove,
You are the one who gives me flight.

I thank you with sincerity,
For giving me such purpose,
'Tis a sacred bond between you and me,
My darling sweetly scented rose.

I Am With You

I have been with you,
Since the beginning,
From when your soul was bright and new,
Before to Earth you came descending,
Showering you with all of my love,
My precious jewel from Heaven above.

I was with you on your day of birth,
My tiny treasure, perfect and innocent,
My beloved light of unlimited worth
You are made from my love, perfect and luminescent.
Feel me showering you with all of my love,
My precious jewel from Heaven above.

When you sleep in the stillness of night,
I am right here by your side,
Cradling you close through till morning light,
Holding you in my strong arms with pride,
Showering you with all of my love,
My precious jewel from Heaven above.

I am here with you now,
My sweetest bright star,
Feel my love flow,
All around you, never far,
Showering you with all of my love,
My precious jewel from Heaven above.

I will never leave you, wherever you are,
Because in truth you are in only one place,
Held closely in my arms,
Resting your head upon my heart,
That is showering you with all of my love,
My precious jewel from Heaven above.

All the ones you have loved, all the ones that you will,
I hold them close to my heart still.
I cradle you all my children of light,
My glorious gifts of heavenly sight,
Showering you with all of my love,
My precious jewels from Heaven above.

Beyond this form and powerful illusion,
Feel this truth burning through your confusion,
You are one with me in the light and love of home,
Bathing in bliss where all shine as one,
And I am showering you with all of my love,
My precious jewel from Heaven above.

Hush now sweetest darling child,
Feel me around you as I bathe you in peace,
Holding you always with love gentle and mild,
Let me fill you with love as your cares you release.
I am with you, showering you with all of my love,
And all is well, my precious jewel from Heaven above.

I Love You

Softly, in the night,
I caress your sleeping form,
My presence oh so slight,
I'm with you through till dawn.
Because I love you.

When tempest strikes the Earth,
When floods rage through the plains,
So greatly do I see your worth,
That I am with you all the same.
Because I love you.

When you sit and feel alone,
I am with you all the time,
When you wish you could come home,
Remember you are mine.
And I love you.

If all the world should crumble,
To dust and faded memory,
I'd see your light and feel humble,
That such beauty could have come from me,
Because I love you.

If you should ever forget,
That I shine with you now,
I'll stay and whisper yet,
So you remember somehow,
That I love you.

If ancient worlds collide,
And galaxies implode,
If hurt reigns fooled by pride,
I shall bear your load,
And show you how I love you.

When all has turned to dust,
To ashen faces in the dark,
When mighty temples rust,
And my presence leaves no mark,
Still, I love you.

If you could only see me,
And feel my heart swell with pride,
Whenever you choose freely,
To know that Heaven abides,
In your heart, because I love you.

Then maybe you would stop,
Losing sight of the higher view,
Because the penny would drop,
I'm never leaving you.
Because always and forever, I love you.

You are my heart,
You are all I am,
I could not even start,
To show you all my plan,
But it is all because I love you.

When you feel lost,
Hurting and afraid,
Remember whatever the cost,
That you can rest in Heaven's glade,
Because I love you.

Immortal

When the Sun begins to rise,
In Heaven's crimson firmament,
A fire alights the turquoise skies,
The wonder of creation's ornament.

Immortal.

This holy stamp of eternity,
Is reflected in our souls,
This blood-red fire is a part of you and me,
As all are one great whole.

Immortal

This is your divine essence,
That part is made of light,
Infinite layers of transcendence,
Unspeakable, timeless might.

Immortal.

This body just a willing vessel,
To traverse illusion and dream,
Still made of stardust eternal,
To house love's glorious beam.

Immortal

The peacock's feather falls in silence,
Through timelessness and void,
Seeing truth beyond pretence,
Our solemn night destroyed.

Immortal

Take leave of caring inside the dream,
Of limitation in a never-ending skyline,
There's God inside this softly stitched seam,
Of body hiding light sublime.

Immortal

Where all your fears run amok,
Within your sweetly painted sorrows.
Blinded titans ancient as rock,
That will see all of our tomorrows.

Immortal

You are made of purest love,
A light that shines forever.
Fruit from the trees of Heaven's grove,
A gift perfect beyond all measure.

Immortal

Infinite star and point of light,
Shining through the ages,
Boundless in stature and epic in might,
A tale of unlimited pages.

Immortal

A spark that holds against the night,
That cannot be destroyed.
A picture given divinity's sight,
An eternal warrior deployed.

Immortal

Your truth, and mine beyond this form,
In timeless wisdom embalmed,
Divine, unending love in a storm,
That leads to perpetual calm.

Immortal.

In-Between Spaces

In between spaces,
An Angel's breath uncovers,
Timeless joy in distant places,
Newfound laughter my heart discovers.

I raise my cup aloft, to sunlit sky.
My arms are open in unblemished reception.
It matters not the where or the why,
I only feel a loving devotion.

The light that pours forth into my vessel,
Is so high and bright I lose my ground.
I can only brace myself, in love, to settle,
As Angels, singing in my heart, resound.

The silent patter of newborn thoughts,
Brighter than a thousand suns,
The fabric of this dream is wrought,
With echoes of that bliss in one.

And so I lay me down inside a hazy meadow,
Gently sighing in a bed of simple reeds,
Lifted far beyond all shadow,
I have so much more than I could ever need.

In Silvery Moonlight

My hand reaches out,
Into the silvery moonlight.
In quiet stillness,
I reflect on my heart's inner sight.

I feel the loss of moment's that never were.
I shed light tears for visions surrendered to the dark night.
I fill my cup with unlimited consequence,
And in between lost instances, I feel my might.

Where have I been? To a place that never was.
Where am I going? Back to where we already are.
What will I do when I realise I am here already, because
There is only one place in golden harmony's star?

As the silvery light embalms my hand,
And not even a cricket speaks out in this quiet haven,
I gaze into the serene light of our Grandmother,
And I feel my soul carried on the wings of the Raven.

To a place so still and filled with silent anticipation.
'Hush, sweetest child you are coming home,
In your warm and safe room, we lit a fire of expectation,
And you can rest cosy when your strange dream is done.'

What treasure have you uncovered in this landscape of dreams?
What diamond dust truths have seeped through thoughts7 crystal clear?
What sapphire wrought moments have shone past lifetimes at sea,

As you've struggled in a teacup, to sail the ocean that is we?

Lift up your oars, and jump overboard,
Or just let your cup dissolve, it is a limiting vessel.
Open your heart and let lightness fill your soul's gourd,
Merge with your ocean, at one yet so special.

I stop in an eternal instant, savouring the stillness,
To see Grandmother's light illuminate the desert,
Where a lush balm of joy delivers such richness,
That I can feel my secrets to wisdom convert.

Beyond the silver light on my willing hand outstretched,
Lie timeless instances of infinity's dreams,
And though to my small thought it might seem far-fetched,
I know that nothing is quite as it seems.

Underneath these visions limitlessly expressed,
There is only love bound within now.
There is only one truth, for which we are blessed,
And deep in our stillness, we understand the 'how'.

Innocent

You always do your best my sweet rose,
That's the only thing you can do,
No matter how good or bad you chose,
You had to do what seemed best to you.
You see, you are innocent.

When people hurt each other,
And act on fear thoughts full of hate,
When brother turns on brother,
To change it's never too late.
Because we are all innocent.

Your essence is pure love divine,
Your natural state perfection,
But clouds can block the light that shines,
When we suffer thought contamination.
But remember we are all innocent.

If confused thoughts cloud your truth,
And you act in a way that's unloving,
Don't judge yourself, let your heart be soothed,
You are doing your best and that's unchanging.
Because you are innocent.

Hear this now deep in your soul,
You make the best choice you can,
To do otherwise is impossible!
No matter what trouble you began.
Because you are innocent.

When we see that if things go wrong,
It only means we are lost in thoughts impure,
We no longer hear the divine love song,
That is always there, you can be sure.

It's just that we are innocent.

Innocently acting on misguided thinking,
Contaminated minds stumbling blindly in the dark,
Forgotten grace without an inkling,
That love is the only thing that can leave a mark
Yes, we are all innocent.

So if you can accept my words,
Then please read on, beloved light.
I trust what's next will not disturb,
I hope to impart some more insight.

Let us now start with the golden fact,
Forgive the person,
Not the act!

The blind beggar in the street,
Innocent.
The youth who steals his bowl and stamps on his feet,
Innocent.

The husband shouting at his wife,
Innocent.
The one who holds resentment for all her life,
Innocent.

Forgetting that you are love and blaming your beloved,
Innocent.
The day when from love to judgment you moved,
Innocent.

The one who seeks to steal your money,
Innocent.
The bear that eats the mountain honey,
Innocent.

The teacher who abuses the pupil,
Innocent.
The one whose anger makes him ill,
Innocent.

The farm worker stamping on the baby animal's head,
Innocent.
The one who beat her and left her for dead,
Innocent.

The one who detonates his body,
Innocent.
The one who lies to sell a story,
Innocent.

Are you still here my words to read?
If you still are I give thanks indeed!

Please remember the golden rule-
Forgive the person who was ego's mad fool.
Bad actions are misguided by contaminated thought,
Because true thought comes from love that need not be sought.

Forgive the person, not the act,
We are all divine light and that is a fact.
So when your sister or brother does something unloving,
They are doing the best they know how so please be forgiving,
Yes, we are all innocent.

Innocent divinity,
Beautiful light,
We are heavenly light beams,
Lost in deep dreams.

Lake of Knowledge

Inside your heart, beating so fast,
Beyond your form, silent and vast,
There stirs a gentle, yet mighty lake,
That holds the answer to all the choices you make.

A mountain so high it reaches to Heaven,
Cups lovingly encircling the great lake of knowledge.
It surface still, and pure and even,
Reflecting serenity and an eternal pledge.

To give you all that you could ever need,
To know of love, to sow the seed,
Of a future so beautiful and filled with light,
That you would caress the angels in flight.

Infinite in nature, a sight to behold,
Unlimited beauty and knowing is told,
Within the lake that holds all knowledge as your right,
And gives you all answers and gifts you with sight.

It is within you, and all of us,
The gift of God's wisdom nestled in your heart.
Just let go and give into trust,
And you will connect with the infinite part,

That is you in your essence so divine and pure
That you can feel safe and blissfully secure.
Because you are pure love, gifted with knowing
That reflects in the lake that heaven is showing.

Deep in the stillness a melody of love,
Stirs in the lake beneath the flight of the dove,
That guides us to the peace to which we belong,
From the dazzling chorus of angels in song.

Silent expanse, crystal clear shining
A perfect reflection of Heaven's divining,
A beautiful gift in the heart of every soul,
Infinite wisdom that's part of the whole.

The Matrix of Truth

There is only one space,
Time is an illusion.
There is only one place,
Behind this confusion.

When Eden becomes true,
There will be unlimited destinations,
As we realize our view,
Is an illusory manifestation.

Behind the fabric of the world that we see,
There lies a limitless network of light,
That holds a secret of reality,
For us when we have gained the insight.

That, in fact, there is no time or space,
Because all is one and presides in bliss,
That the universe is a curtain we face,
And we can see a veil it is.

The Matrix of Truth is a network of light,
As fine as billion strands of silk,
That joins all spaces and times in flight,
To the one place that is our divine ilk.

When we can see this infinite web of here,
That stretches across all creation,
We will learn we can be anywhere,
And unlock the mystery of translocation.

In our mind's eye, we will see the Matrix,
And hold in sight our new destination.
We will soar beyond eagle's flight,
And a new place will see our materialization.

The place that in front of your eyes you now see,
Is simply a grand illusion.
You can swap it as easily as you might a DVD,
To see a new movie in motion.

As we reach for the future we will learn,
To travel without needing any fuel to burn,
No planes, trains or automobiles,
We will instantly move over thousands of miles.

To anywhere in creation that we can conceive,
It's simply a matter time,
That we are able to truly see,
We have unlimited movement because we are divine.

When our bodies have grown lighter,
We shall unlock our inner sun,
And so our auras will shine brighter,
As we know the 'Second Secret of One.'

Moment of Peace

Seek a moment of peace,
In an ocean of turmoil,
The poison froth of hatred must cease,
If ego's insanity we are to foil.

Those souls that are tortured by the lie of separation,
Hold counsel with a host of madmen in chains,
Deceived by ideas borne of fear and confusion,
Acting in innocence but completely insane.

These men are our brothers when we see past their form
We all are the same eternal light.
Forgotten by truth they think war is the norm
And that there is no other choice but to look for a fight.

Fooled by an illusion that just seems so real
Some brothers will need many lifetimes to heal.
Their anger and hatred mean they suffer in dissolution,
Drowning helplessly in rage with no hope of resolution.

The time will inevitably come
When we are all united as one,
When the truth of pure love is all we can know.
But until that day comes we must endure this show.

Feed not this hatred made by bewildered islands of fear
So shut down, a misguided innocence that is blind to the light,
That cannot slow down, the divine voice to hear,
That shows us we are love borne of timeless might.

If you must stand and do battle, then do so well
But remember only love can make Heaven from hell.
At such times as emotions have a tumultuous feel,
Remember purest love, is all that is real.

Mother

She waits in the eternal hallway,
Between worlds quietly forgotten,
In infinity's starry corridor,
Lined with gilded promises born of comfort's lost dream.

Her heart opened to ponder,
All the joys of timeless moments past,
And the ecstasy of the re-joining,
That surrounds every point in space and time.

Enveloped in the divine gift of form,
Yet knowing somehow,
That this space does not exist,
That there are no points in time.

This form a vessel for infinity's expression,
A blessed cup filled with divine essence,
This dreamed form to take us through our illusion,
Until we return again to the divine dance.

This expression of beauty inexpressible,
Gently falls as a silent angel's tear,
Trickling iridescent down the great face of creation,
Knowing only love and keeping truth near.

So she glides through the golden throne room,
To the altar of highest hopes offered,
Her place at God's side now to assume,
Her wisdom and light freely proffered.

Wherever we go and whatever we dream,
Our beloved Mother is with us,
Holding our souls in purest love's beam,
Conducting the heavenly chorus.

The love is always there, our being it surrounds,
With golden light and protection from her gentle heart,
She brings Heaven to Earth, her peace now abounds,
She cherishes each one of us, we are never apart.

Our mother would tell us in this moment of truth,
We are beautiful innocence, divine in her eyes,
We need not try to present her with proof,
She will love us forever beneath unending skies.

A Mother's Tears

When I see you lost in pain,
So lost and filled with woe,
I cannot see the same,
As I still love you so.

If you could see me yet,
I hold you in my arms,
For this world is not set,
I know no way to harm.

As I am pure love,
A light within your soul,
Be at peace my sweetest dove,
As one we all are whole.

Be at peace my sweetest mother,
I hold you close and dear,
As one there is no other,
And I am always near.

I love you oh so much,
I'm sorry that I left,
Stay quiet and feel my touch,
And know I love you best.

I couldn't stay behind,
My work down there was done,
I came and filled my time,
I'm always with you Mum.

Though you can't see me there,
I hold your tears of grief,
See deeper and be aware,
Let love give you relief.

This world that holds you fast,
In pain and sadness deep,
The sorrow cannot last,
I'm in your heart to keep.

I thank you with my soul,
So lucky have I been,
But now I am one with whole,
My beautiful, loving queen.

I did not want to hurt,
Your tears shed I share,
I couldn't stay behind,
I had to leave you there.

But now I see that I,
Am part of you forever,
Because I am one with sky,
With lake and forest and river.

You see me all around,
Wherever you may go,
As I am one with God,
In peace and bliss, you know.

I'd say I'll see you soon,
But I see you there right now,
I love you to the moon,
I'm always here somehow.

So feel me in your heart,
I'm flying safe and free,
Then maybe you could start,
To feel the love from me.

Thank you, mother dear,
I know I hurt you so,
But I am always near,
And I'm never going to go.

My Favourite Bench

Sitting on my favourite bench,
In the middle of a dream,
Under the wispy boughs of the willow tree,
By a gently flowing stream.

Waiting to hear the silence,
The truth beyond this form,
Listening for that sweet indifference,
Whether I dream of calm waters or a storm.

The aged stone circle before me,
Centring around a verdigris sundial in the shade,
Is filled with the cracks of constant changes,
That never have been made.

The moss filled crevices so spongy and green,
Soften nature's carpet to delight my steps barefooted,
There is an energy behind it all that cannot quite be seen,
I can feel it come through my feet well rooted.

I dance 'oer the shady crags,
Tickled gently by a baby fern,
It's time for me to shed some bags,
As deeper truth I once more learn.

Perhaps I will take a boat with you,
And sail on down the stream that beckons,
Or should I dance some more, in the valley where eternal love grew?

It's all going to the same place, I have reckoned.

I just want to make my sanctuary a place of beauty,
To shroud my slumber in silken contentment,
How it looks is just for me,
To make a pleasant judgement.

I would only rest here as long as I need,
I could never outstay my time,
For in this space I plant the seed,
That returns me to my home divine.

And so I journey on through time,
In forgotten moments dissipated in the mists of the silent lake,
This space within your heart is mine,
And only love can we intake.

My favourite bench, my sacred space,
I've found you a comfortable place to sleep,
My own special private place,
That in my heart I keep.

That leads me on to endless destinations,
In the sweetly scented grove,
In the cracks between sky and unlimited horizons,
In the one true state of love.

I found it was a good idea,
To sit on you and dream,
So that my truth could reappear-
I am allness, a love-light beam.

Thank you special seat,
Comfortably shaded under silent branches,
In our fondest imaginings again we'll meet,
Inside timeless enlightened instances.

I'll wait with you,
For the setting of our golden sun,
Which we gratefully view,
In the many coloured sunset of one.

Nothing but a Memory

Nothing but memory,
A thought carried through time,
That severs the link,
Between self and divine.

An erroneous thought,
An illusion not real,
That brings hope to nought,
That you can now heal.

The past is the past,
It happened in then,
Release this at last,
It's a case of just when-

You see that this thing,
That happened long ago,
Has clipped your wing,
And bound you in sorrow.

But what is it now?
This truth must you find,
What happened is over,
However unkind.

It is no longer real.
Think for a moment,
Why can't you heal?
And lie with content.

Your wishes and dreams,
Your hopes and your joy,
Are squashed just because
Of the logic you employ.

To process this thought,
That is carried through time,
That holds you a prisoner,
Sweet child of mine-

If you could see,
That this hurt that you keep,
Stops you from being free,
Because it runs so deep.

So listen to your heart,
And know this as truth,
Then might you start,
To gather the proof.

To show you the light,
The truth and the way,
To unlock your might,
On this very day!

A thousand lost thoughts,
Not part of the plan,
When freedom is sought,
Let them all go you can.

We celebrate with love,
As we hold you in light,
As you rise above,
Your self-imposed plight.

Because you have seen,
It's no longer real,
Just kept alive,
By the hurt that you feel.

That fools you to hold,
In pure innocence,
And so are you told,
You can move forward hence!

From these faded dreams,
These nightmares of old,
That no longer exist,
So come back to the fold.

You keep pain alive,
When you carry a thought,
A prisoner through time,
Of hurts that were wrought.

In misguided innocence,
In sadness and pain,
You hold to illusion,
So come home again.

Leave it behind!
It is no longer real.
Then you will find,
Such joy you will feel!

As you understand,
The power of now,
Move forward in love,
Inside you know how.

To transcend the pain,
That locked you in a darkened room,
And so you will gain,
Freedom from the gloom.

As you smash down the walls,
That had blinded your sight,
As all sadness falls,
Away in the light.

Come out of your shell,
You need no longer hide,
In illusory hell,
Love's by your side!

Oh, lamb that was lost,
In love, you are found,
At such a great cost,
Were those memories bound.

But now you are seeing,
That these thoughts trapped in time,
Kept you from feeling,
Your connection divine.

Kept you from you,
Oh, child of light,
This demon we slew,
To reveal your might!

Free from all memory,
Of past hurts long gone,
We hold a ceremony,
Of joyful praise and song!

For you have returned,
To the truth that is you,
As now you have learned,
To live in glorious hue-

Of laughter, love and lightness,
Of joy and of song!
As you gift the world with your brightness,
And bring all along-

In the wake of your love!
You live a new dream,
As you soar with the dove,
That brings peace in a stream-

That flows through all life,
Just waiting to give,
A beautiful life,
For us all to live!

So in freedom rejoice,
Come home and release,
This innocent choice,
Of misguided belief.

You are love born in innocence,
A being of light,
Your nature magnificent!
Peace and joy are your right.

There is no clearer way,
I can say it than this,
Make this the day,
You feel divine kiss!

And soar with the birds,
The eagle, the dove,
And move free of the herd,
On wings made of love.

Origins

Beneath everything there lies one great power,
That grows the tree and opens the flower,
That causes wind and breeze to blow,
And makes Earth's seas and rivers flow.

Behind all things, there is a hidden force,
That emanates from the divine source,
It beats your heart and grows your hair,
It's in us all, it's everywhere!

It is the hidden power of thought,
That makes all created come from nought,
Whether or not you see it makes no difference,
This is divine intelligence.

A mother's milk is perfect made,
For her sweet child whatever its age,
It causes tides to rise and fall,
Ah, the ceaseless wonder of it all!

It makes the Earth spin round the Sun,
It's a presence that cannot be undone,
It's there inside your warming heart,
When newborn life's great blessings start.

It holds in gravity a trillion galaxies,
Over vast expanse of unending skies,
It births uncounted stars to burn so bright,
And bless us with their ancient light.

It gives us unrequited gifts,
The magnificence of consciousness,
The dawn of thought that once did bring,
The first sweet light of awakening.

It's the ever-present silent lake,
From which our essence it did make,
This energy is in every form,
And in the void before the storm.

There is something that you need to know,
That this mighty power's work does show,
You are not the captain of the ship,
You cannot control this mysterious trip.

It's not down to you my gentle dove,
Your life is guided by higher love!
You are a dance of inexplicable beauty,
Choreographed by divine mystery!

The surest route to inner peace,
Is to this flow yourself release,
All you need lies within your soul,
The same great power of the whole.

Your truth is one of perfect light,
A timeless gift of heavenly sight,
You are the one unblemished mind,
Look inside this knowing to find.

Reaching

Reaching out, I stretched the fabric of my mind,
So far it cannot return again, now forever changed.
I saw such light in deep blue skies so kind,
And now my view is upward rearranged.

I soared with starlings in the fuchsia firmament of dusk
And climbed sapphire peaks in Heaven's mantle.
I saw my beloved body is nothing but a husk,
That holds my essence divine and eternal.

I flew with the Eagles, surveying a greater and expanded view.
I bathed in higher light and found peaceful luminescence.
I changed my being with beauty seen anew
And sang for joy in my angel-winged ascendance.

I hovered with the hummingbird, supping the sweetest nectar
From the blossoming thousand petaled roses of creation,
And I saw how all beloved souls may prosper,
As all are joined in blissful station.

Oh how my heart is filled more full than night sky
Divinely framed over the golden Ocean of One!
How joyfully sing angelic hosts that fly,
Gratefully basking in love's eternal sun!

I saw the truth and in that instant, I saw how
Our past can heal as there is only now.
I raised up my simple cup in an instant moment of bliss
And found precious jewels as are felt in divine love's kiss.

Hold with me now this deep-felt gratitude,
That rides on a timeless beam of love,
This is the essential attitude,
That brings the peace of the dove.

Remember all the gifts with which the divine has showered
You, most beautiful child wrought in the diamond pure-light.
This is the secret, with which you stay empowered,
And spread your wings to join the angels in flight.

Return to Golden Sun

Return to Golden Sun,
To the gentle bliss of one.
Return to that silent peace,
And bathe in love's release.

Return to that sacred space,
In beautiful symmetry presiding.
In the Light Garden take your place,
In rainbow light cascading.

Return to gentle perfection,
Floating on the Sea of Truth,
Beyond your ego's perception,
In sunlit oceans smooth.

Return your heart to love,
Guided on an angel's wings,
Soaring with the eagle and the dove,
Where the heavenly choir now sings.

Return your soul to knowing,
Where amber truth filled light,
That purest love is showing,
Where you may now alight.

Return to the crimson twilit mountain,
And heal your heavy heart,
And rest your weary head, beyond illusion's pain,
Wherein divine love embraces its beloved part.

Return now to bliss and safety, where your soul now lies.
Beyond all earthly cares, and innocent cries of harshness,
Your essence dances with heavenly fireflies,
Forever glowing through the darkness.

Return now to your Father proud,
And your loving Mother's embrace.
Angels serenade you aloud,
As holy tears anoint your face.

Return to Golden Sun,
Blessed child of light.
You belong as one,
In God's eternal sight.

Riding on the Tail of a Comet

I'm riding on the tail of a comet,
Through a universe rippling with light.
I'm climbing to Peace Mountain's summit,
And expanding my vision and sight.

I'm skating on the surface of the Sun,
And finding another soul.
I'm feeling how all are one,
Heading towards the same goal.

Through the many coloured heavens I am gliding,
Past temples of love in higher dimensions,
The beauty all around is so stunning,
I find joy in the oncoming fusion.

I'm sailing the Unending Ocean,
On my shining ship of light,
I'm diving into the I AM,
And I am realising my might.

When I see my brothers and sisters,
I look into their soul-window eyes,
And see that God's light glitters,
In their eternal skies.

When I swim in the Silent Lake,
All knowing is there for me,
Whatever I need, I am welcomed to take,
Whatever I would know I can see.

There is no such thing as limitation,
This is ego's fallacy,
As bright shards of God's perfection,
We can all fly free.

Into the space between indigo and crimson,
On the horizon of unending dreams,
Finding the place, dearest loved one,
From whence love, light and bliss forever beams.

Oh, timeless bead of beauty,
In an ocean of perfection,
I am you and you are me,
And we bask in loves one station.

Feel the love in your heart and soul,
And know that this is truth,
We are infinite parts of a whole,
And our very existence is proof.

Sanctuary

I'm soaring over an ocean of light,
Towards the eternal sun on the unending horizon,
My star-borne wings giving me the gift of flight,
I have no need of land to rest on.

I'm skimming the surface of the Eternal Rainbow,
Its graceful arches stretching through infinite skies,
In this bliss filled moment of a joyous now,
Is where my light-being so effortlessly flies.

I'm dancing over golden waves of love,
So dazzling in their light-filled beauty,
Choreographed from divine source above,
A spectacle of joy, the dance of the free.

I'm gently diving into these waters of light,
My entire being filled with hope,
My vision is that of heavenly sight,
And so I shed illusion's rope.

That bound me fast to pain and suffering,
That never was and cannot be,
For the life we see is not the truth of our being,
That I am you and you are me.

I'm swimming enraptured with the mermaid queen,
She sets me free with compassion and kindness,
She jumps so high in these waters filled by love's stream,
She fills my heart with hope and dissolves all sadness.

I'm diving down through endless depths,
To the eternal City of Dreams,
Where that which is not truth, my heart forgets,
Oh my, how these emerald and gold citadels gleam!

I'm guided gently to the city gates,
So massive and made in many colours of light,
Bejewelled with magical stones that dissolve fear and hate,
They open and I am staggered by such a beautiful sight!

Not of towers, nor of structures, but of a heavenly meadow,
Filled with butterflies and hummingbirds dancing on all the flowers that grow,
With colours so transcendently beautiful and glowing,
That all I can feel is peace within growing.

'Welcome home weary traveller' a joyous voice sings,
As I am lifted in waves of pure love,
'You are here with us always' chants the great fairy king,
'Now rest your soul in this divine grove'.

And so I lay me down on the softest bed of wildflowers,
As the grasses sing on love's breeze,
Here I am home where true light empowers,
And so my heart can rest at ease.

To the sound of the gentle brook under the willow, I listen,
Mesmerized by its iridescent display,
As fairies dancing over its surface glisten,
And I am totally at peace on this my one day.

This place lies within, this heavenly sanctuary,
We can all be here whenever we choose to imagine,
Be it ocean or woodland or beautiful prairie,
We are already there and can return once again.

So always remember that hope lies within,
As you are borne of the light.
You are loved so much that words cannot even begin,
To explain of your beauty in the Divine Parent's sight.

You are safe and you are free,
A child of creation.
So just let go, just let it be,
And every moment can become a joyful celebration!

Sapphire Flame

In the sweetest drift of snow,
Beyond the world of dreams, we know,
There forms a sapphire flame of love,
Burning in a sunlit grove.

Weeping, fairies sing with joy,
As fear and doubt, we now destroy,
To lift our souls up to God's grace,
And feel his warm and gentle embrace.

To see beyond this form so still,
To multicoloured layers of love infilled,
With iridescent dew drops skating on the bellflower's petal,
In the dawn of our tomorrows.

Where peace and knowing make our hearts settle,
As we find our own deep truth to follow.
And so we rise to touch soft light,
So humble, yet always burning bright.

As timeless as a long lost sun,
Infinity shows us: all are one.
We know our place, glorious and free,
The Rising Phoenix writes the Christ's tapestry.

Of love, of truth and inner knowing,
Forgiven warriors in mercy showing
A million blossoms softly flowing in midnight breeze,
Such beauty as golden divinity sees.

In every part of all we are,
A silent songbird perched on a star,
Sings a song of wisdom's pearl,
That anoints our conscious might to unfurl.

In the flood of love's innocent sky,
As fuchsia and azure as summer's eve,
Simmering to crimson, a blaze of glory
That holds within our eternal story!

Our essence that which God adores,
Our might to which angels implore,
That we awaken a many-hued diamond of remembrance,
So we may take our place in the heavens hence.

And soar through the universe as an eagle flying home
As one with all we are never alone
Drifting beads of timeless form
Waiting, waiting for the coming dawn.

Silent Knowing

Silent, silent, silent,
Know beyond the void.
Endless choices,
Own the truth,
The mantel of contentment.

Holding light,
Being love,
The listening eagle sighs,
'When all are one,
Then one is all,
And knowing will reply'.

Being love embraced by truth,
A never-ending light,
Envelopes all humanity,
And brings God by your side.

A thousand angels sing to you,
Of truth in love and joy,
That all your cares can now dissolve,
As ego leaves employ.

The tyrant topples from his throne,
Cracked brittle as the night,
That strains to hide the endless light,
That stands in loving might.

That never pauses, never doubts,
Your feelings can't betray,
That once again you stand with God,
The seventh golden ray.

The ray beholds you unto light,
From whence you have returned,
A thousand smiling joyful truths,
Fly formless in the void.

Awaiting birth in sunless kiss,
The newer energy rises,
The holy stage is once more set,
Embracing all as sages.

Silent, silent, silent,
Listening to truth,
Hearing only love,
Your feelings stand as proof.

Silent, silent, silent,
The new dawn has returned,
When all are bathed in golden light,
The warmth for which we've yearned.

Now's the day we can forget,
The falseness that we've learned,
That lies of separation loss,
The oneness has returned.

Silent, silent, silent,
Softly does caress,
The eagle's feather gently falls,
As love guides all to rest.

Silent, silent, silent,
Exquisite whispers form,
From light that shines from Heaven's heart,
The birthing of our dawn.

Silent, silent, silent,
In stillness peace has shown,
That softly in the quietness,
The truth of one is known.

Silver Wings

Inside my dream on silver wings,
Drifting effortlessly aflame,
Soaring through the void, I sing.
Wordless insights call my name.

Awakening to this inner light,
An angel's gift of deeper sight,
Connected to my inner knowing,
I see truths that God is showing.

Golden sun rays of wisdom's silence,
Fill my form with joyful warmth,
I'm found inside eternal sentence,
That speaks of our divine inheritance.

In Heaven's meadow tall grass sways,
In gentle breeze of perfume scented,
I see our light that shines always,
Perfect, beauty long invented.

I lay me down on petals falling, looking to a sky of indigo
I see timeless stars and higher dimensions,
A crystal river of light does flow,
Into iridescent oceans of love's intentions.

Great flocks of songbirds across the heavens journey,
Singing pearlescent light-song into the oneness.
Their many-hued wings reflecting pearls of harmony.
A million threads of infinite 'Allness'

Inside my dream on silver wings,
Into infinite points of light, I glide,
To the place where I see everything
In blissful heart, I now preside.

Looking into warm light golden,
A rainbow wingspan flying through love,
Joyful peace in Heaven's garden,
Perfect beauty in a secret grove.

It is where you are and so am I
For we are gifted with angels' song,
Who into ecstasy now lift and fly
Back to the truth that lies in ONE.

Skyline of Dreams

Waiting in the skyline of dreams,
At peace the Master slumbers,
Searching for the place from whence love beams,
That brings gentle awakening in the soft earth of eternal sunburst.

I sigh, lost to the forgotten kingdom,
An iridescent butterfly fluttering in the winds of infinity,
Seeking blissful reunion,
In the place where you are me.

I would not falter for even an instant,
If you could shine down on me your luminous wingèd rainbow,
And bring me back to that perfect content,
In the place where all that is knowable, I know.

Sit with me beloved light,
On my bench of marble and jade.
I am awash with wonder, for you are a stunningly beautiful sight,
From perfect divine love are you made.

I would not wait another moment,
To celebrate your light,
I would wait for you forever, yet there is no waiting instant,
To see you spread your wings in flight.

Oh divine spark of perfection,
Sweeter than a bead of dew on the eternal rose of Heaven's garden,
I stand with you beyond the veil of illusion,
With love, I soften you when your heart would harden.

'Only love is real', I gently whisper,
'I'm here, I love you more than words can say
Feel me in your heart, for we are always together
I would give you the universe, please get out of the way!'

Understand this light born secret:
I have already given you all of creation,
And when ego dissolves in the light of our spirit,
You awaken with me in heavenly station.

Snowy White Peak

Soaring so gracefully over the forest of pines,
The aromatic freshness piercing my senses,
Bringing me aliveness, awakening the inner light that shines,
Gliding over great valleys, I thrill to see these green expanses.

Freefalling towards the river of white lightning,
Such inexplicable energy crashing over ancient granite,
The power here is almost frightening,
The beauty and richness is exquisite.

And so I land assured of wild adventure,
My eager feet crashing over rainbow pebbles on the river's edge,
I stride forward, my gate so vigorous and sure,
To live this life to its fullest is my most sincere pledge.

I follow the winding paths that caress the mountainside,
Through the emerald forest full of living green shoots,
My heart and soul will be my guide,
That leads me back to my unformed roots.

Night falls and yet I am far from blind,
A host of fireflies shines light on my route,
Their luminous beauty a gift from the higher mind,
The presence that makes miracles come about.

Onward, I travel, what else can I do?
I was made to journey forth,
To look within towards that which is true,
I am one tiny drop in the ocean of source.

The road has been long,
But now my heart lifts,
I am filled with joyful song,
As my consciousness shifts.

I have reached the summit of this snowy white peak,
The air is clear and my senses awaken,
My travels have led me to that which I seek,
My understanding of love is now my foundation.

Temple of Light

Shining stars embedded in the far distant ceiling,
Soaring so high in sculpted light beams.
Projections of love and heavenly feeling,
I remember it now as though it were a dream.

Graceful arches embracing the sky,
Enchanting balconies over infinity's view,
Choirs of Angels flying on high,
Singing such beauty as I ever knew.

Towering pillars of Lapis and Amethyst,
Harnessing light of healing so pure,
I'm trying to see it once more through the mist,
Was I really here? I'm not always sure.

Waterfalls of light cascading in rainbows,
Encircled by fairies and beings of love.
A crystal clear fountain of pure sapphire joy flows,
Throughout these halls where ascended ones move.

Through the centre of the skylight's scared tetrahedron,
Shines down the soul of Sun,
This solar wonder brings deep revelation,
A whisper away from the truth of One.

Saints and masters and beings of light,
Walking through corridors of quartzite perfection.
Angelic ascendants all gathered in flight,
Over shimmering halls of joy and elation.

The grounds that surround this palace of light,
Hold beauty beyond words description.
Crystal gold droplets of honeyed delight,
Resting on the fragrant, blossomed hills of beauty's depiction.

I wandered here in another time and space,
Free from cares in higher contemplation.
Through fields of serenity, I looked to this place,
To find the secret of true love's devotion.

The form of this temple forever will change,
As beyond the form, description can rearrange.
In a dimension of light, we wait for the star,
To take us to the truth that shines from afar.

Yet this truth is only a light beam away,
A prism of love in an ocean of bliss.
Where singing angels in fields of lavender sway,
Their every breath ushering God's divine kiss.

The Temple of Light rises high in Heaven's glade,
Radiating staggering light sublime,
It's eaves of crystal, topaz and Jade,
Shine out a pure light divine.

A gift to all worlds and other dimensions,
Of beauty, light and love.
That serves to dissolve all dark perceptions,
And bring all souls back to their true home above.

Tree of Light

There was a time in golden sun,
Before the scattered journey had begun,
When we all reached into a fountain of bliss,
Enveloped in a waterfall of the sweetest angel's kiss.

Surrounded in this perfection stated,
In rainbow sighs of hummingbirds supping,
Of nectar from a field of love elated,
In safest peace and heartfelt warming.

In one place we knew this perfect love,
A soaring flock of silver starlings chanting,
We existed there, neither below nor above,
A fleeting glimpse of rainbows dancing.

On soft white sands tinged with fuchsia,
Lining an endless expanse of azure delight,
Filling the open skies with gratitude's nectar,
Shimmering fairy wings in iridescent flight.

Such warmth as seen in the unicorn's heart,
Radiating timeless joy and peace.
There was no end to this bliss, or even a start,
A perfect state, that simply is.

Where lush lined lakes of stillness,
Reflected a perfect light,
And gracefully gliding gilded oneness,
Saw angelic hosts in flight.

Eternal light, Oh to feel this peace!
To connect inside and feel release,
From the form in which we all are now enveloped,
That our listless ego's had developed.

Looking past this holy form so 'real',
Swimming with elder dolphins in seas of light to heal,
We can see beyond this bizarre illusion,
We have never left this golden perfection!

We lay there now in fields of unending bliss,
In swaying groves of light trees pearlescent and beautiful.
Our truest state of expansive joy is this,
Joined safely in God's heart we are at one with all.

Undamaged

When I was a lad, no older than seven
I had an experience that was profound.
As I was lifted up into Heaven
And bathed in light without sound.

I was chasing my friend all around his house,
Clambering over furniture with the speed of a mouse,
Laughing for joy with the excitement of a child,
We were typical boys going absolutely wild!

I was catching him up as we sped through each room.
He could sense me breathing down his neck
I was his harbinger of doom!
And the house was a total wreck!

He had to act soon so he slammed a door in my face.
The world stopped in an instant
He had abruptly ended my pace
And the chase that was constant

Was stopped in its tracks, but I had a big issue
As no longer could I breathe
Or use my lung tissue,
Had my diaphragm seized?

I staggered about, gasping 'Help I can't breathe'
To the adults around who stood there helpless.
They did not know how to unweave
The effect of the impact that had left me breathless.

I thought 'That's it I'm going to die!'
The world fell away, and all was dark.
I had passed out, shadow covered my eye,
But then I was given a gift that would mark

My life from then on, that would change everything.
I was surrounded by light that was golden and warm
It penetrated warmth to my core and was so very soothing.
It was absolute bliss, free of all cares and harm.

It was brighter than the Sun, a place of such peace,
I shall never forget this experience gifted,
It was pure love and joy, all cares were released
In God's loving bosom my soul had been lifted.

Just as I had settled into eternal bliss
I began my return journey.
In the light of truth, I had felt true love's kiss
But I would come back and continue my story.

It seemed as though I was lying in bed
Basking in that golden light so warm,
So comfortable and peaceful, I could feel my head,
But the bliss and love held in my form.

I could have laid there forever
I felt so content, still blissful yet,
I had been given a treasure,
I would never forget.

Then I was engulfed by intense pins and needles.
All over my body, they ran.
I still felt no pain and I did not feel feeble.
But my return proper began.

The next thing I noticed was my face on the floor.
It was cold it was hard and I was lying by that door,
That had sent me back from the place where we are,
That is under the surface and is never that far.

I tried to explain to the adults around,
That the truth about God I had just found.
But to understand this they were simply unable,
So I learned to keep my experience under the table.

But never could I ever forget,
That wonderful moment beyond space and time,
Knowing in truth we bask in love yet,
At one in Heaven with our Father divine.

It took me many years to find the solution
To this gift so puzzling yet divine.
Then I realized that this world is illusion,
Beyond which lies the truth so sublime.

When angels conspired to take away my consciousness,
All that was left was the truth
That we live in bliss in a state of oneness,
I was allowed to remember as proof.

So all this stuff that we carry,
Our cares and our woes,
Are illusions we can parry
Into the love that just flows,

Beneath the surface illusion,
In this life of confusion.
We live in a state of magnificence,
And we can return to that state hence.

We are undamaged, we are perfect,
We are beings of light.
We are all parts of God,
Peace and joy are our right

See past these deep dreams,
And know you are love.
This world is not as it seems,
You come from above

You are there right now,
Your essence is divine and pure.
Get quiet and you'll know how,
To return to that state where you are sure,

Of yourself and your being,
Made of glorious light.
The illusion you are seeing,
Hides you from your might.

There is nothing to fear,
Or hurt to hold on,
I bid you hear,
That nothing is wrong!

Only love is real,
So any hurt that you feel,
Is an illusion of ego,
Of which you can let go.

You are perfect, you are light,
Your essence is divine.
He says 'I release you from your plight,
Beloved child of mine.'

Made in God's image,
You are magnificent light.
The hurt and the rage,
Simply aren't right

They do not exist and they never even did.
Only love is what's real, that I learned as a kid.
So awaken to hope, to joy, and to you.
You are glorious light made from God's golden hue.

You are perfect, you are love, completely unflawed.
By God, in the light, you are deeply adored.
Rise out from the dream that is deeply bound in shadow,
Smell the blossom and blooms in Heaven's sweet meadow.

It's where you are now and it's where you have been,
It's where you will go at the end of the dream,
That was made to help to you see that which you are not.
All the pain and the hurt is just such rot!

Go within and sense the truth: You are the light that does shine.
How could such great glory be held in false shrine?
To ego's insanity that would hide God's love sign,
That would keep you held in the dark when you are divine!

Only madness would do this, would keep you entrapped
Would you listen to an inmate that thinks he's a rat?
Would you hear from the fool?
Who thinks that it's cool,

To leave his Father's house,
And slam shut the door
To where it's warm and it's safe
And lie hungry on a cold floor?

All the stuff that feels bad, that's heavy is wrong.
Lift yourself up and hear joyful song,
That is sung by the angels who fly by your side,
Who lift you to Heaven where you effortlessly glide,

Back to the love that you never left.
Where you can bask in light and love that you can reflect,
Where you can feel safe and you can rest.
You are undamaged, child of God, you are simply perfect.

The Unexplainable Truth

I am the light!
Taken form.
A creation of divine sight!
The first ray of sun in a golden dawn.

I am the truth!
Manifested from the formless,
I am infinity's proof,
A being of love that is timeless.

I am miraculous!
Inexplicable beauty!
My essence stupendous!
Spreading love and peace is my duty.

I cannot be defined,
For I am all of Heaven and Earth,
I am God's presence refined,
He puts no limits on my worth.

There is truth beyond form,
In all that we see.
It's a divine dream we think the norm,
The truth is glorious beauty.

I am unlimited essence!
Borne of starlight!
I walk with the prophets,
With love burning bright.

I am an angel of Heaven!
Descended into dreaming,
My spirit and light freely given,
From my heart, love is beaming.

I cannot be explained, quantified or categorized,
I am love and light beyond measure,
A star shining in God's eyes,
A beautiful treasure.

So look past the dream,
With its cares of illusion,
For this is not what it seems,
You are infinity's profusion.

Voice of God

My throat was sore,
And felt so raw,
I suffered it for years,
All because of my fears.

I tried tapping, and tracking,
And some pillow slapping,
Anger releasing gave,
No pain decreasing.

I wondered what this unwelcome pain was,
I really needed to know because,
Something told me from a knowing inside,
I must find out what this raw pain did hide!

One day after I had grown,
When I was up late in my home,
I browsed through a random Facebook page,
And found myself a modern sage!

As though guided my mouse God had,
I found myself listening to Michael Mirdad!
I judged a little that this fellow looked like a sayer of sooths,
But as he spoke I heard only beauty and truth.

I knew I had stumbled upon him with luck,
Unusually for me, I was a little star struck!
When you hear a light-man talking truth,
You know that of God this stands as proof.

His unique teachings like no other,
Next Sunday I listened again to my brother,
He spoke with words of love and light,
And brought me peace interspersed with delight!

He talked that day of God and Christ,
With words that with wisdom and joy had been spliced!
At the close of this beautiful golden oration,
He led an amazing guided meditation!

I drifted deep past space and time,
And made a profound connection divine,
I felt Christ's presence in my heart that day,
And I asked him why my throat hurt in this way?

His voice responded resoundingly clear,
And explained how the pain was of my ego's fear,
'Until you become the Voice of God' He told me,
'Your throat will hurt and you cannot be free'

'A Voice of God?' To myself did I mumble,
'That sounds embarrassingly unhumble!'
'Do not be fooled, it's your ego that is afraid,
What will happen if you use the gifts with which you are made!'

'It is only your ego that has the ability,
'To make you diminish your light and call it humility!
You have to share a God-given gift,
So why not use it to help others' consciousness lift?'

'Receive now healing if you desire,
And I shall dissolve your limiting beliefs in divinely fuelled fire!'
I said 'Yes please, healing from this I would love,
That I might spread my wings and fly free like the dove!'

At that moment, time stood silently still,
And with a powerful vibration, my body did fill,
I knew I had felt something truly life changing,
And that somehow inside was my consciousness rearranging.

Soon after that I began to channel the light,
With poems and blogging and whatever else felt right.
I wrote articles and pieces given as gifts from above,
And finally, I was able to accept God's beautiful love.

I love the direction I have been taken by this experience
There is nothing more beautiful than making a difference
Most of all I love the inspiration for my poetry,
This is poem number 48 that I've written since February.

When a series of events raised my awareness,
With such beauty, it fills me with inexpressible thankfulness.
I will never forget this gift from Jesus Christ,
Who from within my inner light has enticed.

To write to help others holds incredible beauty,
But the biggest beneficiary is lucky old me!
He healed me and gave me an awe-inspiring nod,
It's more than OK to be 'The Voice of God'.

You Are

You are love, you are the light,
A shard of divine, a spark in the night.
Timeless in nature, unlimited in might,
You are the one and the one is your sight.

There is nothing to fight and nothing to force,
Spread your wings into flight, for you are the source.
Holy essence of love, dearest child in golden light adorned,
You are the allness, the rising phoenix reborn.

Enter your sanctuary, of crystal lit caves,
In your inner plane find peace, and know you're adored in the oneness.
There is no treasure as special as you, my beauty to save,
Oh, drop in a luminous ocean of never-ending stillness.

Oh bead on a pearlescent necklace that stretches into infinity,
And adorns the neck of eternity, formless and beautiful.
The hordes of lost sight may try to enter your dream,
Remember that they are not what they seem.

For you are perfection, no struggles ensue,
A supernova reaction, the darkest demon you slew.
Remember your truth, timeless lord, infinite queen,
A willing participant in this most divine dream.

An essence eternal, unending as the night,
Yet pure love embracing the truth that is light.
There is no more sorrow, riven over dark dreams unfolding,

This ends with the now, as in soaring majesty beholding.

A goblet of gold holding one truth so pure,
We are one, in one place, in the now, that's for sure.
Only love is what's real, that sweet innocent feeling,
Turn once more the wheel and move past your heart's healing.

Release your endings in the wind of the twilit desert plains,
And open your arms outstretched to the crimson dawn,
Feel the sweet morning dew moving in from the Crystal Mountains,
Embrace the honey coated dreams of perfection in form.

Know the truth that flies with the eagle's magnificence,
Stride forth with glorious intentions into the Gardens of Joy,
Respect this illusion as perfect divine consequence,
Make now the bright star, as your dream you enjoy.

Section 2

Free flowing poetry

*'Listen to silence.
It has much to say.'*
Rumi

Accepting Light

Soaring over downy clouds of purest white,
The wind in my hair as I ride the Great Eagle,
The azure horizon of evermore fills my vision,
So comforting is this thinnest layer of endless expanse.

Journeying forth without distraction,
To the eternal star that lies at the apex of now and forever.
I am complete,
My cup filled with heady and scented petals from the rose of joy,
I am on my way home.

I feel it now closer than ever,
A tingling excites every fibre of my being,
And so I know beyond knowing,
That the journey is already completed.

So I can rest in my gently rocking hammock
Woven in silken threads of love,
Beneath the ancient Baobab trees in softly whispering night.
How clearly I hear the quiet call of silence
Over the night time chorus,
And I am stunned by the beauty of it all.

A host of luminescent fireflies rise up
Against the indigo firmament above,
Each one a light to guide us home,
So reassuring, these beads of timeless magic rise,
As one with the many billion star lights in the Milky Way above.

Gently I am rocked by my Guardian, Azareal,
Her flowing locks radiating the warmest light,
Her wings a sight of indescribable beauty,
Gently shielding me from the darkness.

And once again I know that all is well,
That nothing is amiss,
That all is as it should be,
Perfectly placed,
And perfectly timed.

Divinity's sparkling symphony rising in waves of perfect love,
The heavenly orchestra,
Angelic, and golden,
Playing the eternal song,
The song of silence.

The key to wisdom,
That unlocks the unspoken embrace of the eternal star,
Shining brighter than a thousand suns,
Warmer than a million gently glowing embers,
From the slowly dying fire of the ages.

The ages that never were,
And that are always here,
In our hearts,
As we rise up and remember,
All that is.

For a quiet moment,
We roll over and stretch out into the unbound dawn,
Just enough to notice its subtle warm and crimson delights,
Waking just long enough to remember who we truly are,
Before we sink softly back and re-enter our dreaming state.

Somehow at peace,
Carrying that sense of safety and completeness into our story,
The eternal song, sung by the Angelic Choir,
Ever-present should we only stop long enough,
To hear its myriad tones of love and joy
That echo in the silent chambers of forever.

We will return home with our beloved brothers and sisters,
We will return home with our beloved enemies,
We are our beloved brother,
We are our beloved sister,
We are our beloved enemies.

We are beloved beyond these feeble words description,
We play out our roles in the theatre of dreams,
We sing so many songs,
All different, all the same.

We dine with the Angels and ancient Gods
In the glistening halls of the Heavenly Temple,
Supping from diamond crystal cups filled with the Elixir of Eternity.
We fly with the angelic host over rainbow's end
To the land of blissful slumber.

Where one day we shall reawaken.
We are eternal light,
Wherever we are, darkness cannot prevail,
And we are everywhere.

Already Perfect

If your night sky is indigo peace,
Gently illumined by silvery stars flickering in ancient remembrance,
I would be your shining comet,
Burning vermillion and gold through your firmament of dreams,
Blazing a trail of glorious awakening,
Igniting your sky with the fires of eternal truth!

Accept this, my gift of transformation,
For you are the ever-burning sun,
Warming the fertile soils,
Of the exquisite rose gardens in the Temple of Bliss.
Your dazzling brilliance blessing all of Heaven and Earth,
With your silent perfection.

So gallantly you have sought out a trillion distant stars
In subtle ceiling of your house of crystal dreams,
Seeking to bring each light into your heart,
That you might brighten your own illusionary night,
Pushing onward, my bravest, sweetest, and most beloved firefly,
That seeks the warmth of long-forgotten sun.
Again and again, you light up your imagined tears of nightmares,
Straining to flee the void of twilit amnesia.

No more dearest light!
For already you are the brightest star
In all of heaven's graceful display.
So perfect, my timeless jewel
In the eternal crystal caves of priceless treasures.

Already I hold you in my heart.
For you are mine, a perfect light, and an unblemished masterpiece,
Hanging beautifully illumined, in the lapis galleries of the pure-love
That exists beyond space, time and matter.
Where your truth is my truth,

And we soar forever enraptured
Upon the wings of the great phoenix.

Hear my message to you my beautiful one:
Seek not to heal a hurt that could never have existed!
For in the mirrored halls of unending illusion,
Never shall you find the doorway to the golden fields,
Where the hummingbird sips the sweetened nectar of bliss,
And the Master of Light beckons you home to your rightful place,
Held so tenderly and closely to my heart,
In our love without end that cannot know sorrows limitation.

Awakening truly from your dream if only for an eternal instant,
Transcend the murky waters that would cloud your holy vision
And swim joyfully in the warm azure lagoon
That cradles the shores of home
With a crystal clear gentleness born of your own sweet mother,
divine, kind, and forever loving.

She looks upon your sweet, gentle countenance
And is dazzled by your shining brilliance!
And so she begs you to see that already you are perfect
In every way that words could ever express,
And beyond to the luminous silken threads of joy
That join you to her open heart.
She whispers unto you :

'Awaken just a little more. Sink into the warm waters
Of the silent lake that resides deep within your soul.
Hush my beloved, make not the slightest sound,
For it is here you will see that you are the eternal light,
That you are perfection and harmony
Dancing on the joyful breeze of forever,
Over the Mountains of Peace
And those beautiful valleys of harmony's tears.

Already you are home, nestled in the loving embrace
Of a Father bursting with pride,
And a Mother more full of love,
Than there is sweet water in all the oceans of creation.

You need not seek,
For there is nothing to find.
Be still my beloved child,
For in the silence you shall find that you are everything.
And far beyond the illusionary hurts of the strangest dream,
You are already perfect and healed.

You already know all there is to know,
So, rest now in this sweet knowing.
Dream some more, for you shall find your sleep is restful.
For you are loved and all is well my perfect light.

Calm Waves of Love Cannot End

Flying over the Eternal Forest,
My angel wings expanding on into the horizon of dreaming,
Feeling the warm winds of love rising to my grateful face,
Such deep content fills my every moment.

You fly with us on into the eternal journey,
Back to the one home that searches for you,
Yet already welcomes you.
So special, you are our cherished delight!

We sing long nights of gratitude for the blessing that is you.
We wait to welcome you blissfully into our arms.
Oh, how we yearn to hold you close!

How we love to enfold our pearlescent and shimmering wings
Around you!
Oh dearest heart, we are spellbound with excitement,
At the very thought of you!
Our souls are enraptured with ecstatic joy for the gift of your light!

A light as great and beautiful as any other in all of creation!
A pure diamond spark of golden perfection,
Drifting joyfully over shimmering waters,
Lit aflame by the setting Sun, so perfect in its crimson completion.

These calm waves of love cannot end,
Just as echoes of the time before,
When we danced together over perfumed fields,
Of wildflowers potent with heavenly nectar,

That filled the cup of forever.

Where we were sent filled with peace and silent expectation,
Into the dawn of hopeful dreaming,
Over the fuchsia tinged peaks,
Of the Mountains of Eternity.

The Daisy

Imagine a simple daisy:
You see this little flower and are pleased by its beauty,
Then you look closer and notice its soft white petals
Each one gently dancing on the breeze,
So delicate,
So transient.

You look more closely at the petals and see its many striations,
You see minute perfection in these details,
Then you are drawn into the golden light emanating from its centre.
Countless pistils and stamens reaching up for life,
Giving of a million glowing grains of pollen,
Each holding the secret essence of life.

You see the perfection of sacred geometry
Reflected in the perfect alignment
Of each part of this tiny flower head,
That reflects an ocean of infinity
Stretching along the azure shores of eternity.

All this in one tiny flower,
A perfect form of God's creation,
Just like you.

All of the flowers needs are perfectly met.
It need not struggle for air or water or nutrients.
All these are bountifully provided.
It need not search for light,
For light is all around it,

Just as it is for you.

Yet you have incarnated in human form.
So rejoice in all these tiny, perfect details,
Delight in the flowers,
The fresh air,
The warm summer breeze,
That carries the scent of lavender and orange blossom.

Appreciate all the little things,
The endless droplets of perfection,
From the unending ocean:

The joy of a smile,
The delight of children at play,
The power of imagination,
The streets lined with flowers,
And look closely to see that they are, in fact, paved with gold.
The warming sun beaming lovingly upon your grateful face.
The gentle waves kissing the smooth sands of the Eternal Island.

Where you come to know your true essence,
And see that you are all these things,
Just as you are all of the stars in the heavens,
And all the colours of the rainbow and more,
Just as you are ancient stardust,
Stopping for a brief sojourn
On our inexplicably beautiful sphere of emerald and royal blue.

Before it continues its eternal journey
Back to the light from whence it freely drifted,

As a cloud of quiet hope,
Glowing magenta in the lost dawn of distant dreaming,
Where all souls, so deeply loved, return to white sands,
Bathed in the golden light where bliss is known.

Stop here and breathe,
Breathe in this shower of gold,
Feel it fill your vessel,
And warm your soul,
And you are home,
In the stillness now, enjoy peace, Beloved Light.

The Dancer and the Dance

A wave of the ocean,
Does not feel separate from the great water.
I am not the poet,
I AM the sonnet.

A branch on the tree,
Knows it is a part of a symphony of leafy boughs,
An individual that is an intricate part of a greater being.
I am not the tree,
I AM a leaf.

A shimmering feather on the hummingbird's wing,
Is beautiful but cannot fly on its own.
I am not the bird,
I AM the feather.

A plane soars through the sky,
A marvel of our intellectual ingenuity,
Yet the intelligence to create this mechanical wonder,
Comes from the silent wisdom born of the Unending Lake.
I am not the pilot,
I AM the plane.

When a million sparkling mayflies,
Dance as a reflection of eternal bliss,
Each little mayfly is as timeless and eternal as the ancient Gods.
Yet act as the one, greater God, a million pearlescent wings
Hovering on the boundary of infinity.
I am not the dancer,

I AM the dance.

Let the ocean take you.
Let the poet express you.
Let the great tree sustain you.
Let the bird lift you.
Let the pilot guide you.
Let the dancer celebrate you.

Deep Waters

In the deepest waters,
Floating in the dream of worlds long past,
Waiting for that rising current,
That brings warmth and the promise of brighter songs.

The great whale glides in silence,
Then lowers its mighty head,
And sings the song of ancient memory,
That holds the record of all that has passed.

His brothers and sisters join as one,
An angelic chorus hidden in the depths,
In the farthest reaches of this dream of form,
These great custodians of closely guarded history,
Who store the records of this world's greatest treasures.

Gifts of light from distant stars,
High beings who honour Earth with their gentle care.
May we find in quiet reflection the truth of these timeless starseeds
Who come to protect this shell of lush green and azure.

That we might be thankful and gasp in wonderment,
At the stunning perfection and beauty,
That is taken care of all around us,
By a loving intelligence beyond mortal understanding.

In the farthest reaches of the great oceans,
We see the timeless essence of all that is,
Reflected in precious jewelled moments,
Suspended in unending waters.

Diving deeper still,
Sinking into the endless depths,
Discovering untold wonders,
And treasures that defy these limited words.
Infinite variety, light within darkness,
Eternal splendour reflected
In the places our limited form cannot venture.

Here we rest together in the outer confines
Of this great dream.
Waiting quietly for the greater sun,
To bring us gently into our cherished awakening.

The Drawing of a Curtain

All harm to others,
And all harm to the self,
Are just the actions of a lost soul,
Trying to find its way back
To that state of pure serenity,
And total security,
The safety and bliss of perfect divine love.

Stop looking for it outside,
Seek only silence,
Only in this peace,
Can you know again,
That perfection you yearn for,
Pine for and search for.

That which you sense as a shrouded memory,
Or maybe more completely.
That which you were once joined with,
That which you will return to.

That which you long to be re-joined with,
Is, in fact, within you and available to you
Right now in this ever-present moment,
And it always will be,
Wherever, and whenever you may be.

There is no need for harm,
For this is an illusion,
Committed in innocence.

Because only love is real.

All there is and all you need,
Is the perfect love you sense,
It is as close as the drawing of a curtain
On a bright summer's day.

It is in all you see,
It is all there is,
It is you,
It is ALL you are.

The Dreamer and the Dream (FOS Version)

The Guitarist may shine alone
In a timeless instance of musical brilliance.
His magnificent, flowing hair like the silvery river of light
That flows through the eternal temple.
Yet the heavenly solo cannot last forever.
The sweet rhythms, strummed with divinity's plectrum,
Must eventually return to the beauty and harmony
That is the band of one.
I am not the Guitarist,
I AM the guitar!

The Wizard raises aloft the ancient amulet,
His time-worn hands holding steady as the foundations of the Earth.
His clear blue eyes belie ageless wisdom and unlimited power.
With the great magic he shall unleash,
He beholds the glory of all creation.
Yet he too shall diminish in the void into formless perfection
In the place where magic is born.
He is not the Wizard,
HE IS the magic!

The hiker may prepare his boots and kit,
The perfect way to conquer nature's magnificent peaks.
He climbs the mountain with unbending intent,
Forging his own path of ascension.
Rejoice, for the Master has returned home,
Returned once again to the peaceful stillness
The centre of blissful oneness that was never left.

He is not the hiker,
HE IS the mountain.

The Gardener may tend the softly swaying blooms in his sanctuary.
Behold, for he has created a reflection of Heaven on Earth!
He remembers the time in the before,
In the place, he still delights,
Where the honeysuckle climbs the Pillars of Forever,
And the thousand petalled Roses of Creation never die,
Their sweetly pungent blooms filling the Perfumery of Eternal Joy.
I am not the gardener,
I AM the garden!

The dreamer dreams her softly rising hopes,
Her divinely born thoughts ushering the whispers of God.
Her golden hair braided in pearls of wisdom,
So quietly subtle, so deeply profound.
Her arms open and receptive, her delicate hands outstretched
To caress the wildflowers that she grew in her meadow of love.
Yet even she must awaken from her slumber,
That stirs so gently on the scent of lavender and rose.
To be once again in the only place that is real,
Where only now alights the heavens with blissful being.
She is not the dreamer,
SHE IS the dream.

Eternal Shore

Waiting on eternity's shoreline,
For the everlasting dawn,
In the silent instant,
Of twilit remembrance.

The peace is deafening!
The stillness captivates my every sense!
And I am whole again.
Then I see it in the distant sky.

Wisps of fuchsia perfection!
A host of angels on that first flight,
Their iridescent wings reflecting the coming sunrise,
On the edge of gentle dreaming.

I brace myself for the indescribable beauty that must surely follow
These wingèd heralds of magnificent dreaming.
There it is, that first crimson ray pierces my very soul,
With gratitude so heartfelt, it shakes my deepest being.

I tremble, my heart a tentative explosion of love in many hues.
And then I hear it,
The first great crashing wave of thought,
Born of the Silent Ocean.

In these waters of golden stillness,
That carry a new world upon gilded crest.
So majestic, as if propelled by the ecstatic joy of the Merpeople,
As they celebrate these new waves of silken love.

Sweeter than the morning dew collected in eternity's crystal cup,
From the great honeysuckle that climbs the lapis pillars,
Of the sacred gateway to the Heavenly Garden,
Where love creates the many shaped palette of all that is.

In timeless moment I release my being unto this wave of light,
And then I know that I am this wave of love,
That blesses all hearts as one in the golden fields of eternal bliss,
Where wanting is a distant dream that never was.

And now, my drifting form so transient as softest plumes of smoke
From the warmly glowing embers of divine incense,
That smoulder so slowly and unhurried,
On the high altar of the Heavenly Temple.

Imbuing the quiet air with scents of rose and neroli,
Is lit aflame! Bursting with ecstatic knowing!
In the full warming of the new sunrise,
In shades of gold, vermillion, cerise and silvery white!

And I am engulfed in this astounding light,
That washes over me and through me,
Igniting every fibre of my being,
With perfection's starlit consequence.

In this eternal moment, my form is overwhelmed,
With simple joy borne of love's sweet truth.
I yield in trust, I know this sunlit tide flows beyond my control,
I cannot know where the light would steer me.

And as my form begins to dissolve,
Reuniting blissfully once again with that which lies beneath,
That everlasting river of love,
That flies through every transient moment.
And every part of the unlimited wholeness.

I find that I am lifted from these gentle flames,
That I would joyfully allow to consume me,
Lifted by that heavenly host of Angels,
Who first awoke into this dawn of fire and eternal love.

Lifted clear into the indigo firmament,
Where I can glide forever,
Amongst eternal starlight,
In the soft vacuum of unending peace.

Being home,
Being one,
Yet being me.

Dancing with fireflies,
'Oer the mossy floor of the great woodland
Of many souls.

Fallen

The mighty Gods, vaster than entire galaxies,
Shed tears of lost innocence
That create great oceans of sadness.
For they remember before they were diminished.
They know they must diminish further,
Before they can return home.
Yet they are as loved as any cherished child could ever be.
They are as beautiful as a field of sweet blossoms,
Sighing for joy in the eternal sunshine.

Flight of the Great White Eagle

A pearl of divine wisdom,
A capsule of golden light,
A bead of sacred knowledge,
Glistening on the feather of the Great White Eagle.

Shining in the breathtakingly beautiful light
Of the soul of the Central Sun,
Reflecting rainbows and myriad tones
Of colours known and yet undiscovered.

An explosion of indescribable beauty,
Filtering down through the dimensions of form,
From the summit of the highest mountain of light,
Where God rests upon his throne made of angel wings.

Sending us all we could ever need,
Giving us love beyond these feeble words' description,
All working in sublime harmony.
We are feathers on the Great White Eagle's wing.

The Eagle soars majestically into the unending horizon,
Merging with vermillion, fuchsia, crimson gold and azure tones
Of the Eternal Memory.
Her flight soars onward towards the Skyline of Dreams.

Silhouetted against a backdrop of timeless perfection.
She is serenaded by a flock of green-gold hummingbirds,
Who glide joyfully into her glittering flight path,
Fresh from the Heavenly Gardens of Joy.

They sprinkle the Eagle Mother's wings with shimmering stardust,
From the Seven Great Ones,
And so her flight is incomprehensible,
Orchestrated from a knowing and power that is as one with God.

She soars on timeless currents of love and ever-gold hope,
On through the holy portal of many coloured lights,
To finally alight in the fields of golden sun rays,
Bathed in the light of eternal bliss.

And there she rests forever at peace,
Surrounded by the iridescent white mountains of timeless beauty,
In fields of white light rays,
Beside the cool clear waters of the Silent Lake,
Clearly reflecting the infinite beauty
Of the many coloured heavens above.

As her feathers bejewelled in blessings,
And the fine silken substance of divine love,
All we had to do was be a part of her great journey,
Our good fortune as one with our divine birthright.

Fly With Me

Fly with me,
Far away,
To a place that we have seen,
On the other side of a dream.

Where the sanctuary,
Of my heart,
Waits with gentle patience,
In Heaven's sunlit meadow.

A place of sweet blessings,
Where hummingbirds sup the golden nectar
Of the Thousand Petalled Lotus,
And the dragonfly dances for joy,
In violet groves of healing flames.

Where I walk with angels,
Across the heavenly bridge,
That links our souls,
In the Fields of Eternal Knowing.

Soar with me,
Across the ageless galaxies,
Through fields of stardust,
As vast as the ancient gods.

Glide with me,
Over the golden waters,
Of the Unending Lake,

So still, so silent.

Finding solace on a softly swaying branch,
Of the Forever Tree,
Where we alight on our singular journey,
With songbirds gracefully chanting the unchanging rhythm,
Of infinity's lost purpose.

I would not seek to find you there,
Nor would I need to,
For you are the eternal light!
The essence of peace that floats quietly on the still waters of forever,
Always there, unmoving.

I would tell you the tale that cannot be told,
Of the constant truth that cannot be altered,
That becomes revealed in the space between waking and dreaming,
In the gap between the sky and the undefinable horizon,
In the twilit echoes of dreams long past and yet to flow,
Upon eternity's gentle river.

Reach with me,
For that single point of light,
Where the stars meet the heavens,
And my heart is warmed,
In the fires of everlasting bliss.

Let us spend a fleeting moment there,
And find that we are joined forever.

The Great Dreamer

The Eternal sits upon his throne wrought of unending universes,
His white beard flowing upon a stream of unseen starlight,
From a billion stars yet unborn,
Forever with us in the unsung passion
Of the Great Dreamer's silent message.

How can he show us the truth that is unshowable?
Or tell us the unwritten tale,
That tells of love's first light beam,
That spark of golden eternity,
That flows through the unformed horizon,
And on to all that dances in gilded perfection,
In the open halls of ageless skies,
In palaces of light forever turning,
In infinity's joyful playground,
Before the Great Dreamer had need of slumber.

He gazes thankful, upon the many coloured dawn,
Feeling rays of golden bliss,
That warm us through our quiet moments,
And guide us into to our unformed essence.

Where we can stop and hear the Dreamer's message,
For he is with us in unbounded joy,
And inexpressible depths of love,
That would saturate the very heavens,
With such proud awakening,
And joyous knowing,
Of the unsung love song,

That flies with the Great White Phoenix,
Whose mighty wings soar over all creation,
Yet also kiss the void,
And fill the cup of eternal allness,
With uncountable sparkling droplets of the first great light.

And so the Great Dreamer is staggered,
By the sheer perfection of all he surveys!
The unbridled beauty of a summer meadow,
Alongside the cool banks of the crystal waters,
Of the eternal river,
Caressed by the sweetened breeze,
That carries the scent of honeysuckle and rose,
And takes his soul,
Back to the Temple of Light,
Where he began his journey,
That happened on the other side of infinity,
Sailing iridescent on the tip of the Silent Eagle's wing.

Yet his staggered amazement is curtailed,
By the simple, clear knowing,
That the void and creation,
Are as one.

The Great Dreamer has dreamed a trillion hazy moments,
Of butterflies dancing in sunlit fields,
Heavily laden with the many shaped flowers,
Of timeless remembrance,
Their dance uplifted by the warm breeze,
Heavy with the scent of nature's bounty,
And blessed with the perfume of Heaven's rose garden,

Where the master sits in quiet contemplation,
On a simple bench of polished walnut,
Under shady boughs on the edge of the Eternal Forest,
In the soft caress of emerald shadows.

Waiting for the awakening,
Of the Great Dreamer who could never sleep,
Yet rests forever in blissful comfort,
Cradling his many cherished blossoms,
From his beloved garden,
That basks in the golden light of eternal summer,
In his crystal meadow,
That captures the vermillion sunset at the end of peaceful rest.

And his great stone monolith,
Absorbing the limitless power and warmth
Of the first and last crimson dawn,
That sets the Silent Lake ablaze
With timeworn instances of long-forgotten innocence,
On the edge of yesterday's dreamscape,
Into the coming of our eternal now.

For he could never abandon his beloved forest,
Nor leave its tender saplings to fend for themselves.
With the greatest care, he nurtures them,
Ensuring they will become the mighty trees,
Of the Eternal Forest,
That bridges the gap between,
Formless bliss,
And joyful form.

He walks the sweetened musky forest trails in every moment,
And shows a love often unnoticed,
That is the eternal truth behind the song of beauty's thankful sigh.

And so the Great Dreamer gathers his trillion dreams,
And continues his resting moments,
That he would cast into the starry firmament,
So that his forest might grow,
And he could gather all around him,
As he puts his roots down into the fertile forest floor,
Enriched by his unexpectant nurturing,
And watered by his tears of thankful happiness.
Knowing the many dreams are become the one great dream,
And he can rest at last.

The Guardian

In the celestial chamber, she waits,
Her long flowing locks a river of golden light,
Her silken gown a tapestry of divinely cherished instants,
Her soft skin glowing with the gentle luminescence of the first light.

And I am left only to ponder,
The indescribable beauty I see before me.
I gasp as she extends her silvery wings,
Two exquisite shrouds of heavenly grace, like curtains of the softest,
sparkling light from the fountain in the Divine Temple.

She reaches for me, I take her hand,
I am bathed in silent warmth and longing is ended.
Upward we soar,
Her graceful angel flight a spectacle only to behold in awe!
Her twin wings now iridescent
As they reflect the many starred curtain of the night,
Where galaxies are birthed and destroyed.

In humblest gratitude I soar with her,
So safe, so cherished as I look upon her gentle, smiling face,
And I can at last surrender again,
As I am returned that purest state of original innocence.
Her radiant locks shine with the golden light of love.
Somehow I know we are everywhere
Yet we are already home, unmoving.

Faster than light we head towards the vermillion sunset,
So vast it engulfs the unending horizon,
This infinite warmth becoming all that is,
Filling my soul's cup with peace and a gentle radiance.

The soft whispers of knowing's quiet light,
Gently leave her perfect lips and fall into my mind,
As I become of no mind,
As I become the one mind.

And I know myself once more:
Perfect light and purest love,
An expression of infinity,
Slowly circling around the heavenly nectar,
That fills the cup of forever.

I am Here

If you were a teardrop
Rolling down the face of eternity,
I would catch you in my cradle made of light,
And sing to you a song of gentle reassurance.

If your heart burst with a thousand golden sunbeams,
I would be your majestic field of sunflowers,
Basking in your precious light in blissful contentment,
Marvelling in awestruck wonderment,
As I beheld your magnificence!

If the Seven Oceans crashed and thundered
In the illusion of this world's turmoil,
I would be your quiet reflection,
That brings still waters.

If all your hopes were spun into the dewy web,
Swaying in the eaves of the Heavenly Temple,
I would be the sapphire dragonfly of transformation,
That is willingly caught in your silken strands of truth.

I am waiting for you here on the summit of the White Mountain,
Watching your beautiful journey.
You are the joyful dance.
I sprinkle your fertile garden,
With droplets of love from the Great Ocean.

Lucid Dreamer

The Master cupped his hands,
To catch the sweetened water,
Cascading down the rocks worn smooth,
By loving bounty of these lands.

The juniper berry gently brushed the tail of the deer,
As it foraged for bounty in the Forest of Eternal Dreaming,
And all was well as the Master headed back down the mountain,
Refreshed and ready
To start again.

His soul sweetened by the holy water,
Would he remember this as he gently fell into slumber?
And dreamed a million worlds under a million stars,
In a sky without end.

Could he really begin again?
How would he know he was in a divine dream?
How would he awaken?
It is not possible to awaken within a dream.
It is possible to become a lucid dreamer.

The lucid dreamer may shine unlimited light,
From the one true source,
Into the dream of a thousand sleeping children.
And he may do so with the greatest care,
For children who are woken up too abruptly,
Can become overwhelmed with fear.

The lucid dreamer may be a loving, gentle parent
A reflection of our one true parent,
Our loving Mother who adores us unconditionally,
Our besotted Father,
Who croons with pride and the deepest love for us.

The lucid dreamer may fall away from lucidity at times,
But once awakened within the dream,
The dreamer cannot long sleep within that dream again.
And for this quiet awakening,
We are grateful beyond word's limited expression.

The Many Coloured Dawn

The white dove spreads its wings and lifts effortlessly,
Into these skies of deepest blue.
The songbird dreams of moments lost,
In the silent viridian Ocean of Infinity.

The nightingale chirrups its quiet delight,
As it feasts
In the bountiful canopy of the Emerald Forest,
Where nothing gives us everything.

The eagle soars majestic,
Towards the eternal gateway,
That is hidden in the vermillion sunset,
Beyond the crystal capped peaks,
Of the Mountains of Gentle Dreaming.

The hawk glides with steadfast purpose,
Seeing all-that-is in the never-ending portrait,
That is painted on the ancient canvas of hope's fond remembrance.
And I am filled with warmth and a quiet gratitude,
That washes over me with all the fullness of eternity's soft urging.

I could not stop this unending tide,
Washed over me by the sapphire sceptre of the Angel king,
That gifts me with treasure and bounty I cannot describe,
From the eternal caves,
That rest beneath the Mountains of Nothing.
Nothing is everything,
Nothing is everything,

Nothing is everything.

Now witness the silent majesty of the Divine Albatross!
Its pearlescent wings spanning all of that, which is formed,
And all that which is unformed.
Form and formless,
Dancing together on the twilit plateau,
Between the void and creation,
Dancing with such sublime beauty,
It makes my heart burst open!

The River of Love surges through my simple vessel,
And I become the truth-
Pure consciousness,
Pure love,
A diamond of such blinding brightness
And unblemished perfection,

That God weeps for joy.
His tears falling silently through the multiverse,
Cascading through endless worlds,
A waterfall of divine Love,
That ignites the oneness in all the colours of creation,
And the Silent Ocean.

His gratitude expressed only by the tidal wave of light
Washing over all of his children and bringing them home,
Back to the one light,
Where angels sing in gentle celebration,
And the Eternal Song fills all souls
In this bejewelled tapestry of love.

'We sing for your beloved children,
Quieten your minds and slow your thoughts,
And you will realise that you already heard us,
That you are always listening,
And you hear our song in every cherished instant of now.
We are astounded by your stunning beauty,
Your unrestrained glory,
And your precious perfection,
Thank you sweetest light!
This we say with the heartfelt love of a heavenly chorus
Bedazzled by your unending splendour!
You honour us,
You delight us!
You amaze us!
Our gratitude is beyond heavenly expression!
We reach out to you, oh divine essence-
As the crimson sunset that the Angel of Hope chases,
Eternally in the horizon of dreams,
On the edge of forever,
In infinity's unending skyline,
Where we meet ourselves,
And at last, find peace.
In mother's sanctuary of marble and lapis lazuli,
In the heavenly rose garden,
On the silent rose quartz balcony,
That faces west on the Shoreline of Evermore,
Where the Children of Light rest contented,
Waiting for the arrival,
Of the many coloured dawn.'

Once Upon a Thought

Endless thoughts,
Popping up,
Inside our heads,
Wherever we go.

We can't control them,
They don't control us,
We can't change them,
They don't have to change us,
They are only thoughts.

A natural phenomenon,
A divine gift,
With which we can shape our world.

Everyone has 'good thoughts',
Everyone has 'bad thoughts',
These thoughts are neither good nor bad,
They are entirely neutral,
Until we decide to act upon them.

We don't have to act upon them,
We can let them float on by,
Like a piece of driftwood floating on a stream.

Most of us don't realise this,
We innocently believe that we must react to all of our thoughts,
We needn't.

So when you slip into a lower mood,
Step back and pause,
Realise that you are simply reacting to lower thoughts,
And remember that you can drop them.

It takes practice,
Even the most enlightened will sometimes forget,
So when you are blessed with this realisation,
That you don't have to react to a thought,
And you still feel low and you still are hurting,
Don't say to yourself 'It's only my thoughts I should know better',
Have compassion for yourself.

You are doing the best you can with the understanding you have.
Understanding will deepen.
Practice gratitude for the understanding you do have!
And when others project their negativity onto you,
Have compassion for them.
They too are doing the best they can,
With the understanding they have.

We all live in the same world.
But we all occupy separate realities.
We are all doing our best.

Right now every single person on the planet,
Holds within them perfect mental health,
They just don't know it.
Well, some do!
It can be you too!

When you understand the true nature of the gift of thought,
You will still drop into lower states,
But you will recover oh so much more quickly.
The illusion of past also affects our mental health,
But that is a story for another time.

One Light in a Million Hues

Sacred moment,
Crystalized drops of starlight,
Bejewelled upon the eagle's wing,
Waiting in the twilit wasteland between formed and formless,
Reaching for the sacred realisation that both are the same.

Timeworn traveller,
Who surfs upon the comet's iridescent tail,
Looking for that eternal instant,
That hovers on the wing of the Heavenly Hummingbird,
Supping the joyful nectar of infinity's jasmine
In the angelic gardens of forever.

Noble albatross,
Whose divine wings of pure white light,
Stretch across the unending horizon,
Reflecting the dazzling brilliance,
Between the vermillion sunset of forever,
That makes my heart leap in earnest amazement,
And the still viridian waters of the Eternal Ocean.

I sit awaiting the moment I can return to my natural state,
Where thought slows to a silent whisper,
That floats wisp-like through the cool musk of ferny fields,
On the ancient floor of the Forest of Evermore.

Where the ancient masters sit enshrined in leafy boughs,
So heavy with amber and turquoise lichens,
As one with this forest of many coloured dreaming,

Knowing only perfect love,
As they patiently levitate through the aeons,
Waiting for us to return home.

Where the angels softly sing the melody of unabashed contentment,
And mermaids swim in golden oceans of silent joy,
Riding the crest of the divine wave of bliss,
Emanating from the one source.

One place, one state,
Beyond time's sweetened illusion,
Basking in blissful completeness,
On the edge of the one light that has a million hues.

A Pearlescent Tear

A pearlescent tear falling through time,
Without even a whisper,
Landing so softly in the Eternal Ocean .
What are we? Formed of matter so transient,
As a wisp of violet smoke,
In the plumes of eternal slumber.

Awaken now! Timeless titan of yesterday's lost innocence,
Awaken to divinity skating on the wings of the phoenix,
That rises majestic on the eternal flames of the infinite!
A power too ancient, deep and silent
To express in feeble words wrought in illusory happenstance.

A cup filled with an ocean-borne of light,
A vessel that holds the luminescence of a thousand suns-
Burning without end.
Brighter than the heartstone of Angelfire,
Higher than the eternal peak of the mountain of the Sky Lords,
Safer than the chosen babe in the arms of the Divine Mother.
We reach for glory outside when unfathomable magnificence
Emanates from within us.

A God that walks the sands of time
O'er the galaxies and dimensions of lost comprehension.
Stretching out into an ocean of gold rippled with fuchsia.
The crimson 'never-end' waits on the other side
Of this horizon of dreams.
And we are thankful in our completion,
On this our day of vast expansion.

Beyond azure shores and indigo skies,
That reach into forever,
On the edge of the Firmament of Always,
Behind this emerald-gilt mask of never-ending tomorrows,
Simplicity sits tranquil, as a pure white dove
Holding the one key that is made of only love.

Reflections on the Silent River

I saw you on the edge of the Silent River,
Staring at your pale reflection,
So distracted by the ripples,
Sent out within your deepest dream.

This pale reflection,
Is only a dream, my love,
Only a shadow of who you are,
You are magnificence!

The blinding sun setting ablaze the firmament,
With hues of crimson, fuchsia, gold and azure!
The rising phoenix igniting the heavens
With its wingèd flames of deepest truth!

You are an infinite reflection of the unlimited being!
The brightest star burning eternally in the highest galaxy!
A shimmering comet speeding across the heavens,
Shining magic and eternal stardust on all it passes.

Step back from the river's edge beloved,
Avert your tired gaze,
Sit with me on our favourite bench,
And let us gaze into the unending horizon.

That you might find yourself,
Waiting in that quiet place,
Where we awaken from our dreams,
And all of creation is ours to celebrate,

Where all that could be know is known,
Where bliss is all-encompassing,
The place we call home.

Look into my eyes
Filled with love burning brighter than a thousand suns,
Here you will find your true reflection,
Here you will find timeless beauty,
Here you will find unmeasurable power,
Here you will find unconditional love,
Here you will find eternal peace,
This reflection is infinity.
This reflection is God.

Fly with angels
Fly with joy
Fly in golden ecstasy
You are home.

Shores of Evermore

I search for you
Where the sun-drenched waters of eternity
Shine iridescent in tones of azure, fuchsia, vermillion and crimson
Promising a love that shall not falter, that expands forever,
As constant as the unending horizon,
That frames these myriad tones of heartfelt peace,
And never-ending love,
More beautiful and sweet than the nectar of honeysuckle,
Trickling oh so softly down the vines
That adorn the Heavenly Temple.

Sighing joyfully and weighted heavily
By the sparkling morning dew drops,
Each one a universe filled with a trillion lights,
Reflecting the great light of the Central Sun,
The Father and Mother of all light,
That sets this morning sheen ablaze in glorious light,
Of the crimson dawn that burns through the heavens,
And fills the indigo firmament of forever
With the light that guides us all home!

Where we await you most Beloved Light!
We gather in many triangles of love,
Around the great fountain of Heaven's highest transmission,
That beams love across the multiverse,
Cascading a rainbow of refracted perfection,
Like sparkling fairy dust, gently floating on a warm breeze,
Over fields of lavender, rose and wildflowers,
Swaying in ecstatic jubilation,

As we welcome you home once again!

We invite you to dance with us here
In this timeless meadow on the edge of eternity.
We are as immortal fireflies
Aglow with the promise of joy and awakened delight!
We dance with all the grace of the angels of beauty,
Weaving light beams upon our many coloured wings!
Showering our light-filled joy through the layers of Heaven,
Unto you, our most highly treasured gifts of light!

For we honour you with every ounce of gratitude
Beaming from our love filled hearts,
As we nestle in the warm bosom of the great light.
For we are with you as we bathe in golden bliss.
Hear our gentle whispers carried on the silent breeze,
For you are already here with us Beloved Light.

Oh, most precious treasure we welcome you!
Take a breath of release and feel your cup filled
With the eternal love that is the truth of who you are.
So gently and tenderly we would awaken you,
If only for a fleeting instant,
For one instant is forever,
And we could only shine our deepest love and sincere appreciation
Upon you, as you gently and softly sink back into your long dream.

Now resting your head on the softest cushion,
Filled with down from angels wings,
That you might float upon the River of Love,
Within this dream awake!

And bring the golden light of a thousand suns into your world,
Forever elevating the Earth back into the light.

Shores of Home

Drifting through silent waters,
My hearts open vessel glides,
Beneath tranquil skies of fading memory,
Before the long sleep is completed.

The moment of awakening so close by,
A joyous instant as old as forever,
I see the silhouette of home's blessed shores,
Framed in beautiful hues of vermillion and fuchsia,
Beneath the unending horizon.

This ship of distant dreaming,
Sails constant, guided by starlight,
Wrought of a billion sparks of eternal glory,
Joined together as one great light, ever present.

Finally, my vessel comes to rest,
It's ageless bough gratefully kissing the pink white sands,
Of my soul's lost heartland.
My bare feet delight this ancient shore, older than time.

And I am home again,
Warmed by the rising Sun,
Of golden promises at last remembered,
On my tranquil beach by azure waters.

Only the gentlest breeze cools my brow,
Now so light and free of care,
I am my ageless self once more,
I am peace eternally complete.

Soaring

Soaring on alabaster wings of divine intention,
I rise up into the higher realms of love and light.
Ascending as does the Holy Phoenix to ignite the very heavens,
With unblemished magnificence!

I am trans-formed, a wicker man burning in the eternal flames.
That set ablaze my heart with passion born of love,
In the never-ending firmament,
Expressed in myriad tones of crimson and fuchsia.

I shall return again, friend.
Though you may not see me as the manifestation of divine light
That languishes before you now,
In ever-present readiness to fly free
Into the void of formless perfection.

Yet it shall be me just as I am now,
For there is only the now in which to search,
For the tail of the eternal dragon.
That strikes out into the night
And illumines the four corners of Heaven,
Birthing new wonders and a billion stars,
Riding joyfully on infinity's crystal arch.

Oh, glorious creation!
Could such beauty ever be surpassed?
All this and more I can be,
A timeless giant reaching across the limitless stretches of galaxies,
Born and destroyed on the wings of eternity's angels.

See my magnificence and open your heart to wonder!
Rise up and face me!
Look me in the eyes.
See my timeless might,
The essence of creation stirs herein.

Listen to the sweet melody of the contented wren
Nesting on the lichen-encrusted branches of the Forever Tree.
Sense the stillness that lights your way.
A connection, a gift so gratefully received.

No, beloved, thank you for being my gift, my joy,
My heart resting gently on a bed of rose petals,
So soft and delicate, the sweet scent
Of a thousand morning dew drops in an ocean of crisp water
Drawn at dawn, from the great honeysuckle
That delights the Akashic gardens.

Yes, beloved, look into my eyes.
Look deeper still!
And find yourself staring back,
With more love
Than is contained in all the Heaven's golden treasury.

Starlight

Starlight, so ancient,
Burning through time,
Magnificent worlds rise and fall,
As temporary moments, folding into a never-ending instant.

The mythical God rides his mighty chariot,
Across the vast expanse of time and space,
Never pausing, never doubting,
His course runs true.

Guided by that same Starlight,
Burning through the aeons,
Burning with magnificent brightness,
Casting a steady light upon civilizations,
That rise and fall, rise and fall, rise and fall.

The great God of ancient manuscript,
Retires from view,
Absorbed himself into that same
Ageless starlight.

Silently burning, this sparkling light,
Reflected in the eyes of each and every soul,
This light that burns unquestioning for a billion years,
This starlight from an ancient light being,

A vast Titan in the eternal skies,
Yet still a tiny pinpoint of light in the unending Allness,
Still a finite physical presence,

Still a mortal shell, housing the ETERNAL LIGHT,
The light of one.
Yet another great shard of God's golden bliss,

This tiny pinpoint of light,
Shining so far away that its billions years old light,
Barely visible to our naked eyes,
Casts it's light upon us
Billions of years after it too has passed into bliss,

A being so long lived it bemuses our comprehension,
Yet no older or younger than you or I,
No further away from you than the buttercup
Shining golden light upon the beautiful child's chin,
No brighter than a fairy carrying a dandelion seed
To fresh green grass,
No vaster than a grain of pollen
Floating on the warm winds of summer.

No more real than this hand that types these words,
Of no greater or lesser substance
Than any other form we think we see,
No more me than you,
No quieter than the crashing oceans,
No louder than the big bang,
Yet another facet of infinite expression.

Timeless light,
Thank you for your beauty.
No less or more beautiful than you or I,
As beautiful as any of God's wonderments,

Such joy riding on your many coloured rays,
Breaking into night sky after night sky after night sky,
On endless worlds peppering the unending horizon.

Countless skies kissed by your timeless perfection,
Grateful for your guidance,
Thankful for your love,
So vastly different to us that it is beyond our comprehension,
Yet not different at all,
Not in any way that is beyond our knowing.

We need not try to know you,
As we are you,
The same energy,
The same light,
Just a different form.

A form is the illusion of difference,
Everything that exists is THE LIGHT,
Darkness is only that which THE LIGHT has not yet illuminated.
We thank you for you countless aeons of illumination.

You are our guide and you are our reminder,
That there is more on Heaven and Earth than can ever be quantified,
So why even try?
You shine your light so cool and silent,
From a place billions of light years away,
And yet you are right here,
Within each and every one of us.

Surrender

So calmly I listen,
The silence is deafening,
The empty space so exquisite,
That my heart bursts open with thankfulness

In the warming sunlight,
I rest in peaceful slumber,
Swaying in a hammock made of many coloured threads
And dreaming a good dream.

In the gentle sea breeze,
The azure waters unfurl upon pink/white sands,
And it is here where I want for nothing,
That I find my peaceful centre.

As the night sky is painted in indigo and light above me,
I gaze into the distant stars unending,
And I am everywhere,
Already home.

Let me bathe in this silent ocean,
And drift without care,
Full of trust and quiet knowing,
 I surrender to these waves made of love.

Take My Hand

Take my hand,
Reaching out from the stars,
In the firmament of silken dreams,
Shrouded in a million points of light,
The message beams:
'I love you and I am here'

Release your cares to me,
And I shall fly you home,
Your heart I fill with golden tears,
The angels sing your song.

The Arc of Infinity,
Pours rainbow crystal rain,
Showering from that special place,
We built together.
As wisdom flows unlimited from the many coloured firmament,
And we dance on the crimson horizon.

I await you with such tender expectation
When will you notice me beloved?
And join me on the unending stairway,
That ascends beside the waterfall of light,
That flows over the crystal rocks from the holy garden,
Of the Temple of Love?

Where the high ones watch over you,
Joining at one with you,
Always with you,

Loving and cherishing you,
Waiting for you to come back home.

We keep your room so clean and cosy
Your favourite things are there just to make your happy space,
But here you want for nothing,
And we are joyful that you are so nearby.

I would not wait for you another moment,
I would wait forever,
Always here, beloved,
Always near, diamond light.

We sing of your bright colours
Beneath the lofty branches of the Tree of Life.
We celebrate your beauty,
We know your truth and it astounds us!

Where would you go next divine jewel?
Wherever you choose,
Whenever you would be
Our fondest love and praises accompany you,
And all is well.

Would you row downstream?
Your oars caressing the rainbow waters, of the River of Love?
May we join you in your special sanctuary?
You are always welcome,
There is only love for you here.

There is no rush, sweetest one,
There is no time, there is only now.
So ascend the lapis steps and join us,
Supping from the Cup of Truth,
Leaning on marble balustrades on the edge of eternity.

You need not wait to join us,
You need not achieve the slightest thing,
You are already here,
With us,
Always.
And you are perfect.

Tears of Heaven

An overgrown garden, long since abandoned
Bursting with colours, of iris and rose.
Beauty is eternal and ever present,
Without our help,
Yet through the gift of creativity, we are blessed,
To create such stunning wonders,
Manifested from the realm of fond imaginings,
That they move angels to tears.

These tears of joy,
Gently rolling down the face of the angel,
Sparkling with eternal light,
Hold an entire galaxy.

Is this how our universe was born?
Through the joyful crying of angels of light?
The tears fall from the face of the divine,
Shining diamond droplets,
Each one an unending ocean,
Each one a world within a world,
Perfect, made from formless perfection.

Silently they fall through eternity,
Frozen moments cascading through time without time,
Sparkling in the golden light of the Eternal Sun.
The Sun reaches its zenith,
And folds light into crimson and fuchsia hues of bliss,
Against the calm backdrop of sky blue and white.
These rays of love meet the angel's tears

And become a cascading waterfall of light.
Divinely refracted rainbows from the very essence of creation.
This creates such staggering beauty
That the heavenly host weeps for bliss.

With a deep gratitude that could never be expressed,
Nor even felt, for this is the bliss of God,
This is the gratitude of the One Light,
Waiting in such sweet and gentle patience,
For all the beautiful colours of light to return,
To the one pure light.

Until then, the Angels will continue to weep,
Silently,
Joyfully,
In gratitude,
Knowing that the lights are already home.

All emanating from the one source,
Yet thankful for this display of such wonder,
And inexplicable beauty,
That the joy it generates
Is beyond anything that could ever be quantified.
It is pure joy, pure bliss, pure light and pure love,
Astounding themselves!

That which is full and complete,
That which cannot grow, expanding.
Perfection growing more perfect,
Infinity expressing itself without end.

The Unwavering Vessel

Sailing steady 'oer the Endless Ocean,
I shall not falter,
My vessel is perfection.

The Scarlet Lady leans forward
Upon the bough wrought of gold and malachite,
Her piercing green eyes twinkling,
With the ancient starlight of a thousand lost suns.
Her gaze focused ahead, unwavering,
Her burning red locks streaming on the salt-laden winds,
As a beacon of strength,
The eternal flame of truth that sets the course.

This timeless expanse of crystal clear dreams,
Fills up my soul with higher intention.

A shoal of mermaids serenades our passage,
Through foaming bliss, they rise up high in delighted celebration.
The eternal light shimmers on their tails with a beautiful luminescence.

I know not where my lady takes me,
I let her take me through these unknown waters,
My trust in her implicit,
She knows the way,
I need not worry,
Nor would I try to guess her process of divination,
Or the compass by which she guides this vessel.

For she has me safe in this crystal ship of eternal vision,
As she guides me into the sunset of gold and crimson,
On the edge of our dreams
Where flights of pure white albatross,
Ignite sky's end with fuchsia reflections of the before-time,
And the breaching horizon leads me,
So sweetly enticed,
To the space between worlds,
Where only love awaits me.

So deeply cherished am I.
How could I even guess the extent of this love?
Higher than the sun-kissed peaks of eternity,
Broader than the azure horizon of forever,
Deeper than the infinite depths in the clear, still waters of the Unending Lake.

Thus all I need do us sit upon these hallowed decks
And feel that place within my heart,
That leads me at last,
To that silent point of rest.
Where angels caress my tired brow,
And awaken me so gently.

'Come my sweetest, most dearly beloved,
Come back now,
To your home,
Rest with us forever more.

You never left us,
And we were with you,
Always.

For never would we leave your side,
Our most precious jewel of softly wrought starlight,
Twinkling in your Mother's eyes of jade and silver,
We behold you unto golden light,
Which beams forth as an unending stream of purest bliss.

We attend you in that peaceful glade of caring,
Where the songbird sings its joyful melody,
Alighted on the lapis branches of the One Great Tree,
On the other side of the quietly fluttering curtain
Woven in silken threads of twilight.

We draw it slowly and with the greatest care,
Hovering on the tips of our toes, so light-footed.
We awaken you gently, we would not startle you precious wonder.
We love you with more light than a thousand burning suns
In the infinite sky of endless galaxies.
We cherish you, oh divine spark!
Oh shining beacon, our greatest treasure!
Our love for you is beyond all measure.

Rest your head upon my lap.
I'll stroke your hair so delicately beloved one,
I'll sing to you of dreams borne in that scented meadow
Where joyful birdsong celebrates our eternal connection,
In the shaded boughs of yesterday's sunlight.
I welcome you home to love

In this expanded sky of pearl-drop clouds,
Offering sweet sanctuary,
In the golden light at rainbow's end.

Your essence is the light and love,
For you are she and him above,
We wait within, always there,
You only have to stop and feel us.

We are right here in the Golden Temple,
For you are the jewel on our highest altar,
Magnificent, gentle, timeless star!

Sweetest gift, we honour you now.
Thank you for being here, our highest light.
We wait to welcome you home,
You are always in our hearts and in our sight.

I would seek a thousand ways to tell you,
And never find the words,
Feel me in your heart,
And I will shine my love through on pure loves' beam
That no barrier could ever defy.

This feeling I give unto you now!
Stay still and breathe,
Feel me
I am here.

My sweetest, most cherished child,
My eternal light, my highest love,
The pride of all my aspirations,
My greatest inspiration,
My every hope,
My beloved diamond raindrop in an ocean of silent wonder!

Wherever you sail,
I carry your ocean upon my wings.

Waiting in Twilight

In the gap between worlds,
I wait for you,
In the ancient twilight,
Where form dissolves,
Where nothingness penetrates,
And permeates my vision and my being.

This world of cares so fragile,
Melting into the unending horizon,
A skyline of such beauty,
Such formless perfection,
A myriad of subtle colours,
Newborn sensory output on the edge of the void.

Will you join me there?
Sit with me on the cool dark rocks,
So smooth and timeworn,
So comforting,
So unyielding.

This darkness is peace,
Beyond your undefined silhouette,
The endless sky emerges,
Gentle pinks, with crimson touches,
Cool blues tinged with golden flame.
Wisps of white clouds, struggling to be,
We started here in the dawn of yesterday,
We return here in the quiet dusk of tomorrow.

And in between the worlds,
We shine with the luminescence of a thousand suns,
In the perfection of now.
Only to return to this silence, this peaceful nothing,
That stands between form and formless.

Yes, beloved brother, I await you here
In the time-scape of forever,
That has no beginning and that never ends
Watching quietly for the first flight of the eagle,
In this new dawn of unlimited horizons.

You took me by surprise,
When I saw you, here already,
Waiting for me!

Then let us rest here together,
In the eternal shade of these silent peaks not easily discerned,
It brings me such joy to wait here with you,
As one eternal star in this skyline of dreams.

Section 3

Sonnets & Haiku

'Live quietly in the moment and see the beauty of all before you. The future will take care of itself.'
Paramahansa Yogananda

The Blessed Isles

I wait for you upon the Blessed Isles,
Preparing the warmest welcome,
For you, my most beloved witness,
To infinity's gentle plight.

Release all of your illusory cares to me,
Allow me to take care of everything,
For I am here for you always,
My honour and delight are found in your service.

I would shine the warming rays of awakening's crimson dawn
Upon your soul, Beloved Light,
That you might find your wandering way back to me
In these scented fields of Elysian memory.

Where the tall grasses sway ever so gently upon the warmest breeze
And upon a bed of Heaven's wildflowers, you may rest your heart
with ease.

The Confines of a Dream

Time
A beginning and end,
A concept pretend,
That cannot exist
As infinity's friend.

Space
A dimension unreal,
A playground to heal,
A dream within bliss,
Where that's all you can feel.

Matter
Light masquerading as form,
An imaginary norm,
To explore a projection,
To weather a storm.

Parameters we created in order to define,
An astounding illusion that is divine.

Falling Rain

Sensory raindrops falling all around,
Shifting my awareness with their pitter-patter sound.
Charging the air with energy,
With freshness, clear and new,
Filling my heart with synergy,
Opening up my view.
So grateful I feel the droplets splash,
Upon my eager, upturned face.
Cleansing my soul with freshness and a dash
Of hope to find that place,
Where we are all connected,
By the current behind the form,
When all life is reflected,
In the love of our new dawn.

Golden Lady

On the edge of forever,
On the twilit plateau,
The Golden Lady is waiting,
For the many coloured dawn.
So patient, she searches the unending horizon,
Looking for that one spark,
That timeless instant of hope,
That quenches her soul's thirst,
Ending the tale of longing,
Told in the storybook of lost dreaming.
That shining beacon,
That will guide her home,
To love's silent knowing,
Where the truth is showing.

The Illusion of Time

Time- a linear non-entity,
The chart that measures history,
The hourglass of every destiny,
The defining measure of you and me,
Is an illusory concept from which we can be free.

God has no beginning or end as God is infinity,
So time cannot exist if you examine this truth carefully,
For time must begin and time has to end finally,
See infinities' loop never-ending unlimitedly,
And realise that only NOW can exist presently.

So if you are haunted by past trauma persistently,
Now understand that this is only a memory,
A thought carried through time and kept alive innocently,
That has no power other than that which you give it mistakenly.

The Key

Not a thing to do,
In pure love's consciousness,
Lies transformation.

A Light to Remember

Where is the Sun?
The many coloured light,
The luminescence of one,
The star shining bright.

I give you Heaven's ornament,
From the dawn of awakening,
To the dusk of contentment,
Beautiful opening, fondest remembering.

From crimson to cerise,
To vermillion to gold,
Against azure sky released,
To the indigo night, the story re-told.

Gently I frolic in your perfumed fields of lavender,
I am with you, your servant, who whispers 'Remember '.

The Ocean of Truth

The Ocean of Truth flows silently across the night sky,
Shrouded only by clouds of contaminated thinking,
Hidden behind the loud clatter of the unreal try,
Always there, eternal, unchanging.

How much longer will you hold off the inevitable tide, Beloved Light?
A timeless instant of surrender is all it takes,
Let the ocean's tide wash over you,
Engulfing you in the promise of ageless starlight.

Just a fleeting moment of quiet,
Be that calm in the eye of the storm,
And you will find the Shoreline
Of Eternal Majesty.

The ocean is within you, stop efforting,
Find it by your search abandoning.

One Energy

We are all the same energy in a different disguise,
We have learned to judge what we see with our eyes,
And so we created a world of confusion,
Because what we see is just an illusion.

Behind every face, every size and every shape,
Shines iridescent beauty, that is timeless perfection in now.
As the divine green-gold hummingbird hovers over the Unending Lake,
Whose shores burst with the many coloured blossoms of God's eternal meadow.

Young or old, an illusion engraved onto the cup of eternity,
Male and female, simply expressions of energy rising into the dreamers' faded memories,
And when we see a different skin colouration,
We see the same light, manifesting another beautiful expression

And so in our dream, we judge that which we perceive
Until in awakening, we see there is only the truth, not what we believe.

Oneness

Beyond the gift that is this hollow shell,
Beneath the river of thought,
Lies the unchanging truth of our being,
Pure consciousness.

This is the energy of pure love,
Inside each and every one of us,
The same beautiful energy,
Because we are all one.

You need not seek it, it is already there,
In the silence, you will know it.
It is this awareness that will change our world,
For in being this pure love you guide others back home.

To remember, do nothing,
Because nothing is everything.

Quietness

Listening to quiet,
In silence tranquil beauty,
All I need is known.

Reflections

I am your mirror,
And you are mine.
We face one another,
And see infinity reflected forever.

There is no beginning and there is no end,
Thus we are beyond the illusion of time.
We see an eternity of beauty,
Unending waves of pure light,
Masquerading as form.

In the greater view,
This life is also a mirror,
And this universe is just one reflection of allness.

There is nothing beyond the realm of possibility
For we are starlit droplets in the Ocean of Infinity.

Seven Stars

We are the Seven
Servants of the Light.
We are suspended in Heaven,
Seven stars shining bright.

We look upon you from above.
We beam you pure love.
To help conflict resolve,
By helping you to evolve.

Our energy is new,
To the Earth plane, it's true.
In the between space that's still,
We send Divine Will.

We bring hope and higher vision.
To bring forth love is our mission.

Sleep Without Sleeping

Sleep without sleeping,
To find the peace that is always.

Dream without dreaming,
To feel what the truth says.

Awaken without waking,
Let beauty flow from your soul.

Know without knowing,
That all are one great whole.

See without looking,
And know golden light.

Hear without hearing,
Chanting angels in flight.

In the space between worlds
Your greatness unfurls.

A Stray Tear

There are no more spaces,
Than there are instants.

There are no more stars,
Than there are grains of sand.

There are no more feelings,
Than there are thoughts.

There are no more endings,
Than there are beginnings.

There is no more everything,
Than there is one.

A stray tear of love,
May ignite both the Heavens and the Earth.

Everything is the same energy and light,
Joined together we fall and rise, so shine bright!

Thank you for your Colours/Colors

When one beautiful light shines,
Through perfect clear crystal,
A myriad of colours is born.
Each one unique,
Each one exquisitely beautiful,
Yet all made of the same light.

When the heavenly chorus,
Of a hundred thousand angels,
Of masters and light beings,
Sing with a multitude of heavenly voices,
Each voice is indescribably beautiful and each voice is unique,
Yet all are the one voice of God.

On Earth, I found a perfect reflection, a place where I belong,
Where we join as one voice, in many colours of light, in a place that's called 'Forest of Song'.

Three Parameters

Time does not exist.
Matter is illusion formed.
Space is false concept.

Transformation

Silently looking inward,
Searching without searching,
For that single point of light,
That one magical thought,
That changes everything,
That creates light in darkness,
That brings joy inspired,
The transformative instant,
That raises us up to a higher potential,
As the gently babbling brook,
Flows without conscious volition,
And becomes the great ocean,
Made of a trillion golden drops,
Of eternal love that never stops.

Unreal World

Azure waters,
Cyan skies,
Inside this beauty,
The Angel flies.

Soft pink shoreline,
Of the silent ocean,
A wordless sign,
That all are one.

Vermillion sunset,
Painting snow-capped peaks
Whispering 'Do not forget,
You are what you seek'.

Now rest beloved, in your wildflower field,
For you are a dreamer, and this world is not real.

I hope you have enjoyed these poems.
Love and Light,
Julian

Recommended resources:

Three Principles Global Community:

http://www.3pgc.org/

Three Principles Foundation:

http://threeprinciplesfoundation.org/

Signposts (Three Principles):

http://www.threeprinciples.co.uk/

Michael Mirdad (Christ Consciousness):

https://www.michaelmirdad.com/

Orin and Daben (Channelled meditations and books):

https://www.orindaben.com/

CPSIA information can be obtained
at www.ICGtesting.com
Printed in the USA
LVOW10s1727151217
559880LV00005B/1076/P